AF605842

Lunar Calendar

Also by Eric Pankey

Vanishments

The History of the Siege

Not Yet Transfigured

Alias

Vestiges: Notes, Responses & Essays

Owl of Minerva

Augury

Crow-Work

Dismantling the Angel

Trace

The Pear as One Example: New and Selected Poems 1984-2008

Reliquaries

Oracle Figures

Cenotaph

The Late Romances

Apocrypha

Heartwood

For the New Year

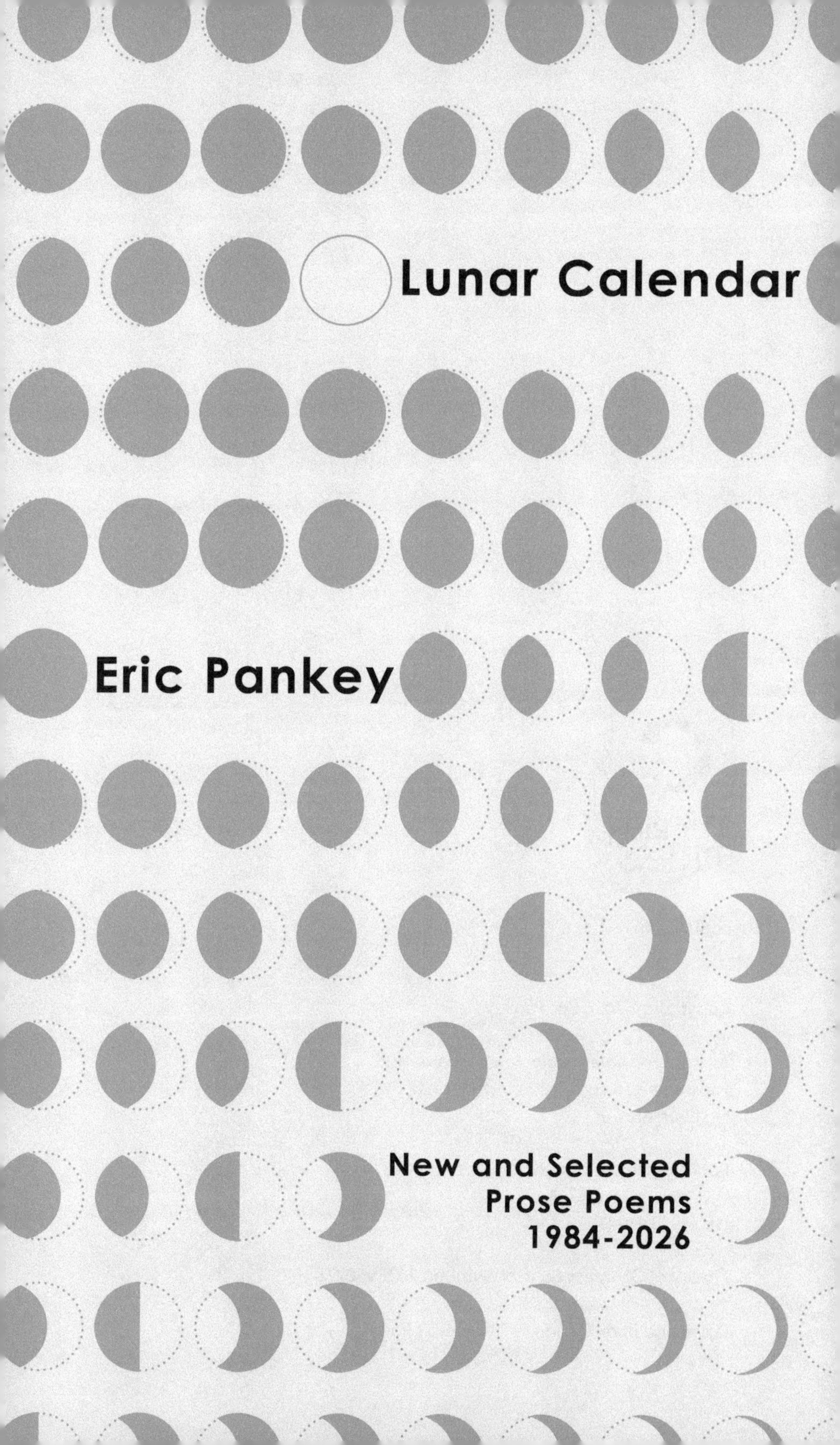
Lunar Calendar
Eric Pankey
New and Selected
Prose Poems
1984-2026

codhill.com

Copyright © 2026 Eric Pankey

All rights reserved under International and
Pan-American copyright conventions.
First Edition

Published in the United States of America

ISBN 978-1-949933-34-5

Library of Congress Control Number: 2025950778

Cover and Book Design by Elizabeth Cline

Advance Praise

It feels like there's more room in this book [of prose poems]—and by that I mean tonal range, but also more room for play, for whimsy, for delight, for memory, and for strangeness. There are still vestiges and themes of what we might call classic Pankey—the desire to identify patterns in the ordinary, to discover the divine, the need to consult the oracle bones, to throw the I-Ching hexagrams—and is there a poet alive, perhaps aside from Charles Wright—with a keener nose for the metaphysical?

–Mark Wagenaar

"Like water, fire, air, memory and earth, these ... poems gather elementally into a revelatory force."

–Rachel Eliza Griffiths

"The poems ... come together to create a landscape both melancholy and utterly beautiful .... Tracing the spiritual as he senses it move through the natural world, he reminds us again and again that to occupy a space is to shape it, and the shaping of experience becomes finally the shaping of the page in language brilliantly wrought."

–Claudia Emerson

Pankey writes poems that give us back, if not the world, our relation to it—where we can learn from what resists understanding, where even withholding reveals, where the future includes all the past, and though the mind might be obliterated by the light it seeks, it seeks it still ....

–Dan Beachy-Quick

"Pankey remains one of our leading practitioners of the metaphysical poem."

–C. Dale Young

"In these precise, dream-like poems, Eric Pankey peers through the clarifying lens of metaphor and parable to meditate on mystery, human sympathy and the divine .... These are such deeply moving, humane, and thoughtful poems."

–Kevin Prufer

"The clarity, intellectual heft, structure, poise, formal dexterity, and music … Pankey has become a poet of formidable skill and achievement."

–Brian Henry

"Marked by an intriguing dialectic of owning and debt, of fullness and absence, of receptiveness and inability, these intense, thoughtful poems trace an arduous spiritual "pilgrimage" of the highest metaphysical order."

–John Taylor

"The voice here is consistent, startling, and carries enough authority to keep us turning pages. Pankey is nimble, even virtuoso, with the meditative mode, and his voice is well-established."

–Matthew Ampleman

"This is an intricate work of decisive oscillation, of tender and careful attention shifting swiftly and precisely between the infinitesimal and the vast, and between one concrete reality and another, without ever losing its way. Such sure-footed writing is astonishing. It would be an understatement to point out that the reader rarely encounters such piercing visionary states, with the author highly alert to sound and syllable, while focused on meaning. Throughout, the author probes our capacity for perception: what do we see (the present), remember (the past), and imagine (the future)? And how do we understand them? What elevates the writing even more is the unmistakable passion and urgency pulsing throughout each of the poem's sections, the deliberate and inspired choice of every word."

–John Yau

For my grandchildren, Karlyn and Ash

What is the source of our first suffering? It lies in our hesitation to speak. It arises from the moment we accumulate silent things within ourselves.

—Gaston Bachelard

Contents

I.

II.

XI
V
II
I
III

I.

Returning in Winter

after Czeslaw Milosz

Think what you will about this place where we have come—light settled on gray silt, the creek bed choked with leaves, a fine mud, the clay of the bank tumbling in.

I cannot remember myself here before, now that it is winter, and the snow begins to fall.

I could believe that without wind the tall, dried grass would continue to lean away.

I could believe that in summer vines tangle the unkept hedges, the red thorns and ripened berries lining the thin green limbs.

I could believe that, yes, I lived here once with you, instructed by nothing I knew enough to remember. I pull my coat around me and listen. There is the cold, the ice creaking in the trees. The clear sound of a world beyond forgiveness.

We were so wise then. We believed cruelty was weather and could change.

How to Sustain the Visionary Mode

Wherever possible, avoid predication: *the night sea, the dark river, this rain.*

As in a dream, where the door opens into a cedar grove, and the haze conjures a screen of sorts onto which an ill-spliced film is projected, and the words, poorly dubbed, seem mere trinkets in a magpie's nest, let each object be itself.

Objects a magpie might hoard.

:The blown dusk-smoke of flies above the sacrifice: The flames inlaid and lacquered: The horizon, a single graphite line on rice paper:

Revelation is and will remain the subject: "Behold, I come quickly: hold fast that which thou hast, that no man take thy crown.

The moment present and full: thyme-sweetened honey, a New World of Gold, quick with what made it.

Let distractedness be an isthmus connecting day to day, dazed with a fume of poppies.

Let the daydream, dimmed by slow rain, slip like a shuttle through the loom's scaffolding.

Let the rain rain all day on the slate, a province of rain, gray as the stone no longer quarried in these hills, gray as the pigeons tucked in the eaves:

The rain, the dark river, this night sea.

Comes a Time

There comes a time when you can no longer believe in the night and its one alibi, believe the snow-light in the orchard, believe the ice at the heart of the onion, believe the fever kindled by hummingbirds and the wind bruised by an angel's fall. There comes a time when the name you have called yourself in hope and in lamentation—*I*—that charred wick, that ruined column that once held up the world—*I*—that incision that never quite healed seems a brittle and makeshift marker for the body that sustained you. Did you believe the struck match purged the air you breathed? Did you believe you were ever poor. Hungry for something more than the little that filled you, day to day? *I*—you start to answer—*I* …, knowing there comes a time.

A Confessional Poem

The story—someday he would have to confess the story—would not resolve itself for the telling; it remained clouded like amber, and, like amber, not clouded exactly, but dense with its own color and hardness, a surface and depth that mimic each other: the light enters it and takes a long time exiting, caught up in the sepia, the golds, the pale yellow of the river willow's leaves, the fog having lifted, but still remnant, a rust stain of iron oxide, the odor that rises from the book as you open it, the dead language of fossils in a jag of limestone, the honey on the blade as it's scraped from the combs. The story, if he tried to tell it now, would move *away* from the causal, like all matter, dark and light, from the trauma of creation.

The Anniversary

The constellation Virgo harbors a black hole at its center, but tonight I see the moon, ordained, a basilica of salt, mouthing its one secret like a saw-whet owl, and all that might be culled, collected, and classified beneath it, named as a disposition of objects, as a taxonomy, an order, a genus, or subject matter is smeared with this salvaged and chalk-dry light, this fine grained and corrosive distillate, this heirloom dust that gathers on the pearl button of the glove, its little satin noose.

: :

When I said, "But tonight I see the moon," I did not tell the whole truth, for I have not even looked outside, but have relied on the conventions of memory, and with a word or two the moon, like a body under siege, wears thin outside my window, the moon forages in the attic, the moon is hauled up like a broken whetstone from a well, for that is what I do with a word or two: avoid scrutiny, avoid measuring the lead weight of my own heart.

Improvisation

The only bridge across Wind River is the wind.

This is not a poem, not a suture of words, not a voice without accompaniment.

The poem is what silence instigates: a sanctuary between "The Temptation" and "The Expulsion" furnished with footfalls and echoes, a way station between *rapture* and *rupture*.

Beneath the chandelier, a single wooden chair with braided velvet cord draped over its arms. The poem is not the chair, but the reconfigured function of the chair: *to be seen*.

The wind rattles around in the heart like a janitor with hours still to go on his shift. And nothing left to clean.

Desire and its generation, its preservation, its fulfillment, its deterioration, its vanquishing, its loss, are the residue of the poem and not its source. When I say *the wind*, I mean *the poem*. When I say *the poem*, I mean *a variable in an equation*. When I say *I*, I mean *a voice without accompaniment.*

No one looking in a goat's eye mistakes it for a human eye. The devil's perhaps. Close enough to be the devil's eye. The little horns and tuft of beard complete the mask. The poem is the expression of the actor behind the mask. The poem is the human eye that, from the theater's back row, seems goat-like in the devil mask.

Put a line through it. X it out: *the wind over the lip of the green bottle. The wind-frayed stamen.*

The Constellations of Autumn

Who oversees this congregation, this collect of caws, this clamor of rooks, gathered by grace around a carcass?

Alas, our narrator is despondent *[from the Latin, despondere, meaning 'solemnly to make a promise']* and having given his word, has nothing else to give.

It is not the rain that set the star-of-Bethlehem white above the valley. Hath the rain a father? It is not the rain, but a hillside of white flowers.

Now is the hour for dousing the fire. The curfew. "Too much whiskey these days, late getting up/I lie and watch the western hills, give up on unfinished poems."

Thomas Merton: "A postulant said this morning, 'How deep do they dig a grave? They have been at it all morning.'"

A sudden wind through the summerhouse. The constellations of autumn. The landscape a box of air, an empty reliquary. Error not erased but crossed out.

Aquinas believes poetry the lowliest of sciences—it has little truth about it. I walk the road and argue with Aquinas. Point out the thistle, the cornflower.

Who would not curse the snake and its shadowy reflection? Who is finding its papery skins snagged in brambles does not begin to believe the Resurrection?

When the roll is called up yonder, when the roll is called up yonder, when the roll is called up yonder, when the roll is called up yonder, I'll be there.

Too much whiskey these days. Late in getting up. I lie and watch the western hills. The sun all haze. Read the poems of my teachers and go back to bed.

Dismantling the Angel

Put each feather, quill point down, in its own Mason jar, sprinkle in paper ash and table salt, and place each jar in a root cellar, refrigerator, or cooler. As one does in an autopsy, make a Y incision from the back of the ears, meeting at the sternum, and then down the chest. There should be no bleeding. Fold back the flesh, which by now will feel like vellum. Remove the heart and liver. You will find no bones and no other organs. You will find the heart where you expect to find it, packed in straw, canvas fibers, millet, and crushed cowry shells. The heart, as dull and heavy as slag, can be used to hold a door open. The liver—green, made of malachite smelted in a coal-fired kiln—can be ground to sand, or dissolved in salt water, distilled, making a whiskey to warm the winter. The appendages—the arms, the legs, and the wing-hinges—are useless and should be stacked with the cordwood. They burn easily but add no heat to the fire, no brilliance to the flame. The little drops remaining on the cutting table look like dried blood but are in fact gall-stained paraffin. Scraped up, melted and recast, they make lousy candles. They are best used as a sealing wax or as a suitable lubricant for pipefittings. If you have not done so, put each feather, quill point down, in its own Mason jar, sprinkle in paper ash and table salt, and place each jar in a root cellar, refrigerator, or cooler. This is important; thus, I repeat myself. Left overnight at room temperature, each feather can regenerate an entire angel, all the feathers a holy host.

The Kingdom of Smoke

A man has two sons. The younger, having asked for and been refused his inheritance, leaves, saying, "If I were to speak one more word, if I were to complete one more sentence, I could not avoid the predicate's tragic turn." Angered, the elder son yells at his brother in farewell, "A crow flies as the crow flies. You are brother now to crows. The crow's curse is its caw, the sweep of its coal-black wing." What is a father to do? Wear his shame like a splint and a sling?

The two halves of his land are divided and held together by a thicket's bent vertebrae.

He drops a match into the thorn-tangle and soon his is a kingdom of smoke. Looking back, the younger son sees the blaze but continues away: a long stretch of road behind him, a longer stretch ahead—wind-worn, sleet-skulked, perhaps impassable.

I admit I was not privy to the garbled argument between the elder son and the father, silhouetted by flames, but I witnessed the dumb-show and shadow-play skirmish of their gestures. Flushed and scattered by fire, crows above the twin fields resolved as an as-of-yet indiscernible genus of randomness.

The Talismanic Shirt

The cotton of the shirt—tight-knit, impenetrable by sunlight, yet somehow airy—did not reveal the thousand and one scriptures inked in minute, almost illegible handwriting on the shirt's inside: down the sleeves, across the back and on either side of the mother of pearl buttons from collar to the tails. Radiant, the shirt shone as if its own source of light. To see the shirt was to be in its presence, to be illuminated by it. Whether the universe opened or closed did not matter. White, if white exists at all, could not be exemplified better than by the shirt. If one opened the illustrated dictionary to white, there would be the shirt in miniature. If one opened the illustrated dictionary to *shirt*, there would be the shirt glowing, glaring, flaring, shining, glistering in miniature. I have worn the shirt. Perhaps to say I have worn the shirt is too common a way to express it. It was not as if I pulled a black turtleneck over my head and watched the play of static, not as if I had put one arm into a blazer and then another as the tailor brushed something off my shoulder to say, there, that's just right. In the shirt, I was neither subject nor object. The shirt on me was the subject and the object. Do not mistake the shirt for some childhood dream of an invisibility cloak. Riddles, enigmas, conundrums and tables open before the shirt, open easily like the shucked paper of a garlic clove beneath the blade. Far from invisible, I stood out in a crowd. Normally polite children pointed. Men and women shielded their eyes as if I were naked, as if I stood there naked and then had become even more naked. The teenagers on the corner couldn't be bothered, which is to say they took note but would not let on to one another. No one envies the wearer of the shirt. The shirt is there: clean, pressed, ready to wear. I gave it up once, which is to say: it is there: clean, pressed, ready to wear. At night in the closet on a common wire hanger, the shirt vibrates like a struck lightning rod. I listen to its low hum. I listen to the swarm of scripture inside the shirt calm as if the late dark were a drowse of smoke.

The Autobiography of Fire

The fire retains only its shape, its shifting, ambiguous, wind-shredded shape.

A bevy of flames. Sparks splayed beneath a sledgehammer. Bonfires at midsummer. Pentecostal tongues. Banked embers. *Meteors fright the fixed stars of heaven.* The charred body of Osiris as spent fuel. Signal fire built from a shipwreck. A thumb-struck match flaring. A fire kindled with Cain's offering.

Although the flames rise and reach as high as the top of the stake, someone in the crowd feels the need not to beg for mercy, but to call for the condemned witch's death as if it were not at hand.

Prior to words, the inarticulateness of fire, a long, mumbled sentence through the hardwood forest, down the mountain, to the seaside dunes, where it shushed it way through the sparse grasses.

][brimstone and *fire* from the LORD out of heaven][he took the *fire* in his hand, and knife][Behold the *fire* and the wood: but where is the lamb for a burnt offering][in a flame of *fire* out of the midst of a bush][the bush burned with *fire*, and the bush was not consumed][the *fire* ran along upon the ground][and *fire* mingled with the hail, very grievous][with *fire*, and unleavened bread; and with bitter herbs][

Having consumed the Library at Alexandria, the flames remained tongue-tied, mute. Fire like poppies in the wheat. Poppies like fire in the wheat.

][his eyes were as a flame of *fire*][like unto a flame of *fire*][gold tried in the *fire*, that thou mayest be rich][seven lamps of *fire*][And the angel took the censer, and filled it with *fire* of the altar][and *fire* mingled with blood][a great mountain burning with *fire*][having breastplates of *fire*, and of jacinth, and brimstone][by the *fire*, and by the smoke, and by the brimstone, which issued out of their mouths][

The fire retains only its shape, its shifting, ambiguous, wind-shredded shape.

The Parable of the Empty Jar

A certain woman carried a jar full of milled grain. While she was walking on the road, still some distance from home, one of the handles of the jar broke and the grain emptied out behind her on the road. When she reached her house, she set the jar down and found it empty. As she set out again to fill the broken jar, she noticed a flock of birds lined all along the road feeding. From her house to the mill where she had purchased the grain, one bird after another took flight before her footsteps.

"I've never seen birds feed with such a hunger," she said to the miller as he refilled her jar and took her coins.

"A cold winter must be coming," he said, "as cold as hell."

"I thought hell was a fiery pit," she said.

"It is," he replied, "but we feel it as ice to our marrow. Imagine how it would be for the birds which are hollow-boned."

As she walked home, the grain spilled and one bird after another landed behind her to feed. When she reached her house, she set the jar down and found it empty. There was no wood in the stove, no oil in the lamp. The cupboards held only dust.

"A cold winter, indeed," she said as she started down the road to the mill, this time wrapped in a shawl, and the flock twisted up before her like a pillar of smoke.

Essay on Mannerism

Not a cave's absolute dark, but more like char, ash-scrim, the chirr and clicks of starlings, dusk-tinged, a crag of coal, this black we call black as if a word might be offered as proxy: black like the petrified heart of a lamb, like the posture of grief the figure embodies in Rosso Fiorentino's 1521 "Deposition"—hunched, hunkered, harrowed—with his (her?) back to the cross.

Essay on a Lemon

Like a lens, the lemon clarifies by way of distortion. Like a mirror, the lemon implies an unseen onlooker. The lemon, transformed by one's attention to it, is a spark pent up in a barn, is tenuous auroral light, is long shadows on a glacier. The lemon waits to be recognized like the inscrutable event of a miracle. The lemon is like a nail before the hammer's invention. One experiences the mystical as the phenomenal. Note how easily, with the vessel of the body broken, one ascends. The lemon is an anagram, a quicksilver sliver of memory, countless sparrows alighting on a swimming stag's rack. Like Man Ray's "Indestructible Object," the lemon had to be remade. To make one is really quite easy: "Cut out the eye from a photograph of one who has been loved but is seen no more. Attach the eye to the pendulum of a metronome and regulate the weight to suit the tempo desired. Keep going to the limit of endurance. With a hammer well-aimed, try to destroy the whole at a single blow."

Lunar Calendar

The moon is a midwife, who delivers a bundle of salt.

The moon sheds a spring-fed light, white as the limestone in
Galena, Illinois.

The moon is a knuckle gashed to the bone.

The moon rescinds its blessing, rests its forehead on
a crosier of walrus ivory.

The moon is magnetite, a precipitate of iron and oxygen.

The moon is Junebug larva.

The moon snags the train of its wedding dress in the blackberry
brambles.

The moon is the underbelly of a mole: lame, hobbled, all maw.

The moon inhales the cloy of opium, exhales gypsum dust.

The moon is a geode, a glacial erratic, a sinkhole.

The moon is a window opaque with reflection.

The moon, fluent in every tongue, remains mum.

The Equilibrium of a Swan's Feather

Alive, no doubt, with the low voltage that runs through a dowsing rod, the swan relinquishes its swan-ness. The swan vanishes. Or, at least, on the continuum of visible light, the what-was pulses ultraviolet. One might, in response, write an equation regarding the pull of parallel distances, of one disembodied notion upon another. One word salvaged from the obsolete, maybe two, might be all that is needed, (if *need* can be used here to mean *desire*) to offset the swan-reflection where the swan is no more.

Film Still

after Douglas Gordon

As if on the surface of the moon, cold in light and shadow, time itself is outmoded—all glints, struck flints, mica flares—like TV static, the fluorescent hum of the exit booth in long term parking, or at the turnpike's end, and if the future seems permeated with foreboding, imagine the landscape unfurling behind, a blurry rear-projection, without soundtrack, without the windshield wipers' tick, or the on-again, off-again rain, imagine the driver's eye as dark water down a drain and the past seems a momentary misdeed, a modicum, a mote washed away by a tear.

Two Children
Threatened by a Nightingale

after Max Ernst

Attentive as one is to a whisper, the children wade through standing water, uncertain of its depth or source. They find and salvage a sogged train schedule. For their short lives, the depot has been boarded shut. He has a flair for death and can fashion a noose from corn silk. She keeps an archive of diaries. She is the movie extra a camera seeks out, lingers on. He reads the subtitles aloud before the characters speak. She imagines sleep to be a furnished room. He imagines rain on the rolled hay, the must of empty stables, the tin-edge of blood on the tongue. By schema and classifications, they are a sister and a brother. Waylaid between this puddle and the next, she creates a theory of the spectral. He fingers through a cache of candies. He is plump and ready for the oven. She could not even flavor a stockpot. She is the overlooked subject. She deciphers a language of mis-hearings. They cling to the hitherto unknown. When they dissect the bird, they find nothing of the song.

Owl

Owl (oul) n. [ME owle<OE ule] 1. Rain on a scythe. 2. A hem of water around one's waist. 3. Autumn marked by an X if X can equal the renunciation of memory or that which is impervious to interpretation. 4. A seed placed on the tongue of the deceased. 5. Sparks splayed beneath a sledge <Through the blacksmith shop the owl flew.> 6. The way the divine penetrates the material. 7. The experience of loss although nothing is missing; mute stupor; black bile. 8. A discarded yet imperishable garment snagged on a branch. <Look, there is an owl in the sycamore.>

The Blindfold

I wear a blindfold, and I close my eyes. The dark is darker that way. That sound, like a rowboat in fog, is the attic fan. I try not to imagine the dust it blows around. If a room assumes the identity of those who inhabit it, this is my mother's room, or rather the room of my mother's ghost. By force of habit, the charred tree blooms in the yard. I do not see it. I am blindfolded. I catch in the air a scent like chalk erasers clapped together, the little plume that rises to the school janitor's nose and causes him to sneeze. How neatly he refolds his handkerchief and slips it into the unbuttoned pocket of his khaki work-shirt. My mother's ghost lights up a cigarette. A little shred of tobacco clings to her lip. She licks her finger and touches the hot iron. The bottom of the cast iron frying pan is white with the congealed fat of last night's steaks. On the TV, a gentleman vampire waits a long time before opening the door to the uninvited guest.

Perhaps you find the blindfold an affectation. But only when I wear the blindfold and close my eyes do I hear the static of towels lift from the basket, breathe an air of steam and starch, feel her brush past on some task, humming "Moon River" or "Sugartown."

Essay on Compassion

I caught a fox in a Havahart trap. When I went to release him, he hunched, hissed, snapped, let out a yelp, and bared his teeth, defending the corner I'd put him in. He stunk with a blunt odor of musk and myrrh, a hint of shit. I had to shake him out of the cage with more violence and intimacy than I'd have preferred.

Ars Poetica

The first people watch the drama of their fireside shadows and, even before the camp-following wolves lose their voices, the ritual sharing and eating of food replaces sacrifice

A forethought

A scrutiny before words

How easily words un-name

Slip like skin from a blanched peach

A yoke, a hand-carved wooden device, joins together a pair of draft animals, especially oxen. It consists of a crosspiece with two bow-shaped pieces, each enclosing the head of an animal. The yoke is a tool to harness and focus energy, to allow the two draft animals to work efficiently together toward a singular end, often plowing or hauling heavy loads. Jesus, the son of a carpenter, who said *For my yoke is easy, and my burden is light*, would have known that the more perfectly fitted the yoke was to the oxen the more easily the particular animals could take advantage of the tool rather than struggle against it. The purpose of a well-made tool is that it eases and lightens work

Sand is heated to glass and lenses are ground,

Thus, distance is bridged, or the otherwise invisible magnified

It goes, we say, *without saying*. Nonetheless we say it.

Souvenir de Voyage

What does one call a tree reduced by fire to mineral? The quarry walls—tool-marked, wind-pitted—hold the last of first light on their scree-riddled edges. Stones excavated here were carved as columns, crowned with stylized acanthus leaves. Absent the whole, the part suffices. The edge of the Luberon is the same color as the tongue of a prairie rattler: a blue flash at bright noon.

: :

An image emerges from, disappears into, light. From the ruined half-arch of an aqueduct, one imagines the distance coursed, the water's silvery shimmer like a struck string. A sudden gust of wind bangs a shutter. A spider, almost translucent, crosses an olive leaf. Hypnos bears a bouquet of poppies through a city built upon the air of its own name. Light again makes of a room a dwelling.

: :

I possess, I admit, a limited repertoire of themes and motifs. A hot breeze through the vineyard. Vines heavy with fruit still weeks from ripeness. In the middle distance: haze upon which, in the background, a mountain floats. I look up and I am a sickly boy again: writing an edifying dictum one hundred times in chalk. A white-on-green cursive alphabet runs the length of the blackboard.

: :

As night lifts up out of the valley, one stone-girded terrace at a time, and the rows of the vineyard and limestone grit of the goat and sheep paths submerge into the shallow surface of dusk, one recalls the weight of touch it takes to make a mark on paper, the pencil sharp, precarious, prone to breaking. The first mark is the horizon. Should the next intersect or run parallel?

: :

Upon a prone monolith—what will soon be repurposed as a tomb cover—figures crowd the depthless black niche of Caravaggio's "The Deposition." One man, holding Jesus by the knees looks outside the frame for consolation. Overcome, we say, by grief. The pain mounts, but that is not the worst. It burrows in. One *becomes* grief—a stone in its stoniness, a worked lithic edge.

: :

The stone wall stands more tumble and ruin than wall. If not for a stretch of flawless mason work, around which everything has fallen, one might have thought this load of rocks dumped here raw material for a new wall. Hard to imagine lifting each stone, turning it over and over in one's hands, attempting to puzzle it into place, never mind the scrapes, the backache, the wall, at last, standing.

: :

Beyond where the iron tracks bisect, steam lifts off the horses' backs. A dragonfly with mica wings hovers somehow, then darts. Farther down in the valley, a little fog broods. Each version of this tale highlights a different impediment. If the cicadas ever let up, one might hear a grub as it burrows beneath the tarry pine bark, or a green lizard skitter across the limestone gravel.

: :

A ghost, like a flame, is the shape of its consumption. A ghost exudes cold, and one feels the change in the air as the ghost comes and goes. What one senses is experienced as a glimpse, a glimpse that outlives its moment. In the same way, a redacted text can disclose by its very withholding. The realm of God is like leaven, which a woman took and hid in three measures of flour.

: :

Here a child plays a game at dusk: she drops a pebble into a stone trough, disturbs the line of silt settled there at the bottom. Magritte says, *What resists our understanding lends a radiance to what we think we see*. Before dropping another pebble, the girl waits for the silt to resettle. In that time, an ordinary wall beyond her is transformed by light, but the change, one might say, is imperceptible.

: :

Woke to the sound of horse hooves on cobbles, but from the window saw nothing but the vertical plume of cypresses, a glitter of green among the olives' dry leaves, how beneath the clothes' damp weight the line slumps. Went downstairs to the parlor, where an old sofa and unused piano convalesce, and looked out from there: only a tacked-up torn poster for a circus that never arrived.

: :

To look up at the stars is to experience the past as present, ancient light cast for future eyes, and this is that future: starless, cloud covered. In the dark kitchen: the cold shine of a dented kettle, nectarines, fresh from the market, aglow, spectral. When a car climbs the hill, a riotous gesticulation of shadows plays across the wall and ceiling. The power's out. If you pace your steps, lightning lights a way.

: :

Above the narrow-streeted village: ivories and grays of an overcast sky. To seek, avoid seeking. The church bells ring, yet hours elongate, hours foreshorten. The world is assembled in ocher and charcoal on cave walls. So little time between the dew-bent fern and peat, peat and lignite, lignite and anthracite. To evoke enigma, place two objects next to one another and step away.

: :

The poem is not a referent for experience, but an experience. The poem is a scale model of an invented place, an aggregate image, suffused, as an empty room is, with the various selves that occupied it and never returned. Yet desire and memory remain there like dust exposed on light-sensitive paper. Come. Enter as an arson investigator might into the aftermath of a light-obliterated space.

: :

Between a day that's ended and the one beginning: a narrow passage outside time. Don't expect to find there votaries of a vestigial cult of Dionysus, twin falcons rending the flank of a gazelle, or a shroud of jade squares held together with copper wire. There you'll find what Humphry Davy calls the *intimate actions of bodies upon each other, by which their appearance is altered, their identity destroyed.*

: :

The cold, greenish umber of a storm piles up. You are surprised, as when your host reached out to join hands and offer thanks for the food you were about to eat, the food she had prepared. The cold, greenish umber of a storm piles up and, where the mountains should be, a crisscross of lightning. *I have not made a habit of gratitude*, you think. Then the thunder, more delayed than you might have imagined.

: :

The ladder snake, our household god, prefers the cool beneath the stone stoop. She need not lift her head to note who has entered, who has gone. Emitting negative luminosity, she enthralls the mantis, rhinoceros beetle, and the vole. They offer themselves as sacrifice. As befits a god, she has removed herself, keeps her own counsel. She speaks, when she speaks, in sibilant parables.

: :

Evening star like a keyhole into a barely lit room. The garden sparrow surveys its dominion. Except for a quartered lemon on a blue plate, the outdoor table is cleared. Those gathered are strangers to one another. Each has a room that faces the garden. They tell stories remote and practiced enough to sound true. As dark comes on, their gestures grow animated.

: :

Remnants of iron give jade its greenish hue. The yellow bough apple casts lavender shade. You find, instead of a map on the table, sheaves of scribbled field notes: *Exit where you find habit still shadowed by the sacramental. Turn where wind fords the river.* You crank the winch and haul up a bucket slung with water. After the sloshing settles, you look into the water. Not even your face is reflected there.

: :

The crag on which it's perched gives the church a melancholy disposition. The ruin, long quarried for building stones, open as it is to the elements, might not even contain the sacred. *Why not,* you have asked yourself again and again, *just turn away from the formless infinite, from the god-inflected sublime?* It is as if you have stepped into a clearing when your eyes had adjusted at last to the forest dark.

: :

Last night in a dream, you opened the armoire and found it to be a weathered harp case, and the harp, strung with chicken-wire, swung on hinges like a make-shift screen door. Sometimes, the edge of things can only be seen when looked at obliquely. Beyond the open door: the sound of rain in the dry, overgrown cherry orchard. Last year's cherries remain: wizened, rusted, unplundered.

: :

In Velazquez's painting "St. John the Evangelist on the Island of Patmos," John holds in his right hand a white quill—all but a few barbs plucked from its shaft—as he prepares to write in the blank book slumped over his left forearm and right thigh. He looks off and up to the right at some commotion in the clouds. The realm of God is like a field of crows heard long before it is happened upon.

: :

A storm dusts up and passes quickly. Lightning, a consuming blankness, leaps from the ground to the clouds then down again. Acrid ozone. Little corposant flares here and there to graph what fire fathers forth: this botch the demiurge calls *creation*. You have prayed to evade the incessant hum of thought. You have prayed for the angels to be silent so the unnaming might begin.

: :

To be god-filled is to be enthusiastic. *When a dot begins to move and become a line*, Paul Klee writes, *this requires time*. Things are what they seem to be: blood on the butcher's apron, plaster marred with scrawls and scratches, distance the deep cloud-shadow veils and discloses. In the old tales, the pursued mortals transmute into heady flora, into the diffuse light of constellations.

: :

A displaced object becomes charged with enigma. Placed in a vitrine, a specimen jar, or archive box, the ordinary thing, now displayed and separate, safe from dust, from theft, from the merciless light, seems precious, vulnerable, and unattainable. Add now other objects, displayed in some irrational arrangement or in serried ranks. The viewer will perceive an organizing principle.

: :

The landscape, framed by my fourth-floor window—fields, vineyards, orchards—gleans the last luster of light. From this distance: the ruled stillness of a garden, the stroke of an hour prolonged. If not for the repetitions and tallies, this inquiry, as unstable as dust, would not proceed further. Memory, like a net, is more negative space than positive. For all the bounty, what has slipped through?

: :

As soon as we become motionless, Bachelard says, *we are elsewhere; we are dreaming in a world that is immense.* I observed a vine as it let go of its wire. Each day the vine pushes further: spills across the furrow and onto the field's rough edge near the rocky, gravelly path I follow. A ripe cluster of green translucent grapes dragged along. As in a dream. Now, without trespass, within reach.

The Last Sunday in Lent

In Sunday school, a girl watches the wind outside the windows inhabit the dark shape of pines. The girl considers the unsayable name of God. She, too, has a name no one has spoken, or dares speak. Sometimes it is sweet on her tongue like hard candy. Sometimes it burns like an ember. She dips a slender paintbrush into a jar of water and writes—no one watches—her secret name in water on the linoleum floor. The other children practice signing as they sing "This Little Light of Mine." The girl watches the name evaporate, and thinks, *my light is not so little.*

Another Reading

As her client, you are given the sturdiest wooden chair, the chair on which a hanged man once stood. You sit down on the scuff where his heel had kicked and skittered away the chair. She is a palmist and claims the lines on your hands read: *The marvelous is born from refusal.* Her shop looks out onto the stage of a piazza. It is Ash Wednesday. In drizzle, a carny stands beside a collapsed canvas tent, as blue cotton candy melts down his forearm. You ask for another reading. *This time*, you say, *let me first take off my gloves.*

Melancholia

On the periodic table, it is the densest of elements. It does not refract or reflect but absorbs all light. On the tongue, it has no taste at all. All day the rain falls in its room. All night the rain. Mold blackens the walls. Drops slip from the ceiling and, in a future not yet imaginable, stalactites and stalagmites begin to grow, barring the door, the windows. A poor cousin to gold and lead, it never quite sleeps, is never quite roused. It averts its eyes like a beggar. It broods on the dull edge of its brooding, on an arrival again postponed.

Parable with my Father as a Boy

He woke at an hour the church bells no longer strike. At that porous border between night and morning, he gleaned windfall, russet to rose, all pocked and blemished, and pressed it to a winey, tin-edged cider. He foraged for seeds and nuts, dug up tubers. Hung the whitetail from the rafters and slit its throat; its blood tick-tocked into a galvanized pail.

All this before his sisters woke and pestered him: *Why has the milk soured? Is that the Adversary stealing our nanny goat? Only yesterday, while you napped, he sowed tares in the field!*

A Public Education

The boy was abandoned, not raised, by wolves. For his first three years, he suckled what he could to get by: a fox, a star-nosed mole, a skunk, a nanny goat. As an adult, tossing back the last of a martini he would say, *Milk is for babies and barbarians.* To stay warm, the boy rubbed two sticks together. The boy rode an old broke-down mare to school through a blizzard. No saddle. No saddle blanket. He'd say, *A horse's heart is as blue as a glacier's.* From page four of his *Eclectic First Reader*, the boy read aloud to the empty schoolroom:

> *The two boys run fast.*
>
> *They run as fast as they can.*
>
> *One of the boys has no hat.*
>
> *Here is a small dog.*
>
> *He has the boy's hat.*
>
> *The boys cannot catch the dog.*

The boy read that once the universe fit into the space of a jelly jar. The hard part, he figured, was screwing the lid on. Nestled in the hayloft, the boy would listen to the night sounds: sleet in the branches, a distant church bell striking the hour, the wolves loping away from town on the highway's icy, gravelly shoulder. Before he falls asleep, the boy frets about the boy in the story, the one without a hat. *It is winter*, the boy thinks, *he'll catch his death of cold.*

Book of Hours

A jostle of stars at the edge of the Crab Nebula pinpoints the heart of Taurus. Under the right conditions and with a steady hand, you can see it with binoculars. As with most things, the conditions are rarely right, the hand never steady enough.

: :

Snow arrives on the hackles of wolves, but from where? As before the snow, one must see an image for what it is: fugitive, belated. Mute like a river. Like the stupor of smoke when a bell jar is placed over a lit candle. Like a snowflake caught on a sniper's eyelash as he aims.

: :

No homespun melancholy, no traveler's nostalgia, this ennui works its way into the marrow, lodges there, and enters the blood. Thus infected, the chronic effects beginning to show, it is best not to enter the underworld, attempt to lure a shade out of the realm of shades.

: :

All stories begin in the forest and only latter do we move out of its dark to follow the herds, to build with mud and straw. A shimmer of stream through the woods is not enough to lure us back. We were happy: everything still to be done.

: :

A snare of horsehair. Cinders on her cuffs. Blocked access to an exit. Borrowed time. Da Vinci's chapter called *How to Make an Imaginary Animal Look Natural.* Bronze boats afloat on a sea of rice. Spiral galaxy. The palpable pull of gravity.

: :

Odysseus narrates three tales of forgetfulness. As he speaks, he tastes the lotus honey on his tongue, feels the burn of salt in his throat. He has no memory of the past, only memories of the stories he tells, memories of telling the stories.

: :

A fogged-over pond floats above the thawed ground like a monocle. Blue heather and other ruderals take hold in burnt-out places. The viewer, absorbed in viewing, takes note of distortion at the periphery, how straight lines there ache toward curves.

: :

There's no refusing the refuse, the detritus, the accumulations, the scrape of scrap crushed, trashed, deemed useless at last. Of all the subsets of the set of the whole, which is represented by the intersection labeled *a*? Vestiges corrode, cede to rust.

: :

A day moon, silver damascened with iron, shimmers a little. The fields look like fields in a Book of Hours where magpies follow a sower. What he casts down the birds take up. He does not look back. He looks ahead. He is the sower.

: :

A non-native invasive is introduced, or a horse is ridden into a funeral pyre, or you imagine a quantity where counting no longer makes sense, or Jesus, distracted, a little annoyed by their ploy, wastes their time, scrawls magic words in the dust.

: :

Virga above a landscape made distance tactile. Then she spoke the truth. He wanted an explanation. She explained that there is no objectivity—how can one see without the interference of interpretation? He recalled her hesitations, not the words she uttered.

: :

My brother strikes the door slammed on him. To enhance this charm of anger, my brother strikes again the door slammed on him. Not to knock, but to knock it down, break and enter. All he finds inside are swept floors, open cabinets, and empty drawers.

: :

The day the war ends, one notes the lazy way smoke hoists itself up out of the chimneys, how the last of the migrating flocks, drawn elsewhere, spills out of the trees. Some things are known only in transit. One weeps, thus fails to behold the soul exit its body.

: :

What is Italian for its *paltry semblance*, for *the birth of specters and phantoms?* The bird, and not the birdcall, is hidden. While you decide on your order, the waiter caresses the rumpled tablecloth smooth. Each item on the menu has a red line drawn through it.

: :

How does amber preserve a sliver of Baltic light? What is allowed the rose, burdened as it is with significance, its innermost aspects threadbare, worse for wear? Have you, like I, at last been thwarted by the vagaries of circumstances?

: :

Not a single name in the hotel registry. The cage of the elevator waits at an upper floor. The clerk and concierge, you assume, have stepped away for a moment. The buzz of overhead lights evens out the silence. The little bell waits: polished, unrung.

: :

Like the plump bee on the hollyhock, or the garter snake sunning on slate, one is merely a lodger here. Swifts trace elaborate spirals above a ruined chapel with four winds as walls. A muddy wheel rut, full of last night's rain, gleams.

: :

A lead plumb holds the vertical. The alchemical glyph for *lead* is the scythe of Saturn. Saturn's heart, cut into, gleams a moment like lead. It is sweet as well touched to the tongue. On the periodic table, lead is the last of the stable elements.

: :

The hiss and crack of quick-burning tinder. The piano and its cabinet of hammers. The sound of a mountain waterfall through dense forest. A leather bellow's asthmatic huff. A sudden clatter outside like an avalanche of axes.

: :

"Surely, a time will come when on those frontiers, a farmer, as he ploughs with his curved blade, will turn up ancient javelins eaten away with flaky rust, or will strike with his heavy hoe empty helmets, and marvel at giants' bones in the upturned graves."

: :

How does the nightingale extricate itself from night? What is the word that means *that which could not have been conceived of at the outset?* Why did she smile when we called her honesty *ruthless?* How does the green shoot break through the bark inaudibly?

: :

Like the candle a midwife bears at a tragedy's end. Like sparrows all winter weaving shrouds. Like the bloat and draggle of a body caught in a deluge. Like the tarnished tin of a stagnant pool. Like a pack of jackals asleep among the tombs.

: :

River mist lifts in the middle distance and the bridge beyond, foundered in fog, submerges into background. How else to read the bluish gray expanse across a deeper bone-soot gray, the arcana of crosshatches, smudges, and ink smears?

: :

The lodger, lost, consults the logic of the ant's seemingly aimless to and fro. On his face, moonlight falls, fits as easily as a death mask. The fire sings from its ring of rocks. Wind hews the drifts of grit. The lodger wears an open wound called *brevity.*

Trouble in Mind

An overlay of shadows and shade. Crows in the winter corn. The goldenrod flame-like. The body of Jesus translated into the body of Christ. The lid of the Shaker box fits so snuggly that when it's replaced, the air inside sighs. The net floats like a cloud, the skein's interstices: bright points. A sea of negative space. She was a beautiful girl. From the depths of the pinewood, how does one imagine the idea of *a clearing?* Always a swarm of images at hand waiting to inhabit the framed mirror. By *poverty,* I meant the poverty of language. You thought it all so Romantic: the craggy knolls, the tumbledown shacks, and bosky hillsides. At the party, one entertains doubts. Did you say a *cursory personality* or *a personal curiosity?* Did she ask *how to avoid the void?* In a single day: a retrospective of weathers. The hanged man afloat between two worlds. I have spent my life contemplating the play of light upon an interior: the complexity of perception, the perception of complexity. You watch a thought transmute into *a thought of watching a thought.* Tugged at, a circle expands to an ellipse. A marriage of dusk-light and pearl. A plate of cherries to feed those in a lifeboat. A thousand ooliths. She was a beautiful girl and, she said, that's where her trouble started.

Sanctuary

I am familiar with the impurity of recollection, the errors in continuity, the fleeting glimpse easily claimed as witness, the kind of ill-lit moment a photograph might hoard. I live, as you do, between contingency and control, between presence and distance. Let's call this *the year a child washed up on shore*. You saw the image as I did, repeatedly on the news and in the paper, the little one face down on the waterline's saturated sand. Yet nothing disturbed the moth's reign over the night. Nothing healed the tree peppered with hundreds of weeping woodpecker holes. Nothing bleached out a dye of turmeric and iron oxide. In the Bible there are two parallel narratives of mass infanticide. The first foretelling the second. The second recalling the first. The child does not writhe or jerk. The child does not shiver beneath its wet clothes. The child, held still in an extended moment of composed stillness, is dead.

Variations on Hadrian's "Animula"

Sun bright, but a thaw hard to imagine. A snow-saddled erratic dominates the clearing. Curves of blue drifts conceal a tumbled stonewall. The brook under ice is tannic with oak leaves. *Why art thou cast down, O my soul? And why art thou disquieted in me?* I *recall* I say, but in truth call after. *After*, belatedly. So much thrown out, trampled underfoot. If only words were salt—soluble, savory, vital, electric. Belatedly, I call after. Late spring. The whole sky foxed with stars. The soul: taut, tuned, like a viol—polished, baroque—old fashioned, out of style, a kept keepsake. Crisp with trampled mint, at once preamble and postlude to chance, to change, wind shuffles honeysuckle, exposes a rusted snarl of barbed wire, a rotted post. The soul like a thrown voice, a voice thrown. Clouds pile up all morning for a storm. Or so it seems. *Little soul, errant spark, lost wanderer—O, indweller—you have flown, and I grow numb, wan, melancholy, pallid, bereaved, a shell, a shucked husk, emptiness as evidence of your* once-presence. Each new line crossed out. Each old line crossed out. Such satisfaction in the setting down and the crossing out. *O my soul, kin and stranger, wayward guest, waylaid spirit, charm and figment, flame and tear, silvery shiver and cold tremble, belatedly, I call after.* The day begins as always in the dark, then light leaches through, reveals rooftops and walls, an offshore island, its black pines slashed with a gash of gold. How to account for such abundance?

The Work of Poetry *or* An Imaginary Pane of Glass Parallel to Sea Level

It takes so little: a ball of twine, a stick, and box to make a trap; an inkblot on folded paper to render two bears pursued by a dragon, (or is that the moon propped and slumped on twin crutches?); a sharp edge to engrave a mask a dancer might wear to court the rain; the upper quarter of a stone sphere to set a shallow dome above a shallow pit, lit and aglow with the feeble light and dull warmth of an ossuary; a bed of nails on which to rest a sheet of glass.

On the Occasion of the Release of *The Senate Torture Report*

In Piero della Francesca's "Flagellation of Christ," the room is needlessly spacious for the blunt work at hand. Three figures in the foreground take no notice of the violence. Except for the purpose of composition, they are superfluous. Some critics argue these three are Nicodemus, Joseph of Arimathea, and the beloved disciple John, who will later bribe the authorities, claim the body of their friend, and bury him in a borrowed grave once the humiliations, beatings, and execution end. At this distance, Jesus appears to console his tormenter, whose right hand is raised (one can barely see the whip) as if in protest. Who has not been like this man who beats another man and feels put upon?

Alias

Like everyone he passed on the street, he entered the world nameless. Names attached themselves to him: *José, Albert, Cornelius, Jake, Tyrone, Søren* .... He wore each easily like a well-tailored coat. He would take it off at night, place it upon a hanger, and in the morning emerge with a new name from the closet. The names multiplied. His lovers each with his or her own endearment: *My Lamb, Little Neptune, Sugar Pie, Pale Ramon* .... And the children at the bus stop, who called out tauntingly, *Uncle* or *Boo* or *Señor Zoobeck*. Recognized, he would tip his hat. To some, he was a mail carrier. To some, a bookie. To some, he was the dapper pensioner, ivory-handled cane in hand, who strolled each evening around the plaza in Vejer de la Frontera. To some, he was the last of the Czar's tragic family. *I* could not stand in for his many heteronyms, but *I* is what he called himself at night in his prayers to God, as he had as a boy, at that time, still nameless—unmoored, anchorless, adrift—a pronoun without an antecedent.

Outtakes from *The Newlywed Game*

In the crowd around the victim, she is the one who admonishes: Give this poor person room to breathe. He prefers a tender touch to an apology. She thinks he is the one who should apologize. They first met, he says, because he sensed the gaze of an unknown viewer. They met, she says, because she had always wanted to be a contestant on *The Newlywed Game*. She insists that none of the resurrection sightings are authentic but are a manifestation of a group hallucination that moved like a contagion among Jesus' followers in their grief. Fair enough, he responds, noting in his daybook yet another non sequitur on her part. Regarding *making woopie*, she compares it to an algorithm that collapses into randomness. He compares it to the water's surface: fugitive, ethereal, a depth without reflection. She shakes her head *no* and says, you mean it is like a fog illumined from within, aglow yet opaque. Yeah, he says. What she said.

The Other Story about José

after Carlos Drummond de Andrade

Jill, hoping to spice things up, suggests to her husband, Kevin, that they invite Helen to join them for a threesome. Helen, while flattered, feels such an appeal from her immediate supervisor inappropriate and reports Jill to the Office of Equity and Diversity Services. Ted, a senior manager at the Office of Equity and Diversity Services, is asked to investigate the charge and finds, much to his dismay, that he is infatuated with Jill, and although she is fired, he finds ways to continue to bump into her. He begins to attend her church. Ted works with Kevin, Jill's husband, decorating the church for Advent. As they are hanging the Christmas greens, Ted confesses to Kevin his love for Jill, and Kevin, surprised by the revelation, loses his footing and falls from the ladder onto the sanctuary's hardwood floor. Kevin dies. Helen, feeling double remorse for getting Jill fired and, by a direct chain of events, Kevin killed, attends the funeral. Before the night is over, Helen admits to Jill that the only reason she did not join in the threesome was the third party, Kevin. Helen admits her desire for Jill, and they go home that night together, surprised at the fervor of their newfound love. Ted, who continues to stalk Jill, watches through her second story bedroom window as the two women undress. Knowing that the Fates love irony, Ted has asked his friend José to hold the ladder steady, so he—Ted, that is—is not the second man to fall from a ladder in this story. José owes Ted a big favor, thus he stands amid the dark, scratchy shrubbery and holds the ladder. The story of that favor is another story entirely.

Speed Dating

He says, "Sometimes, attended only by my reflection, I squint and feel the drill bit of a headache begin to whir at a low speed behind my right eye, and what I am actually sensing in my peripheral vision is the gravity of interstellar gasses as they flare and contract, condense into a giant planet worthy of a god's name: a ferric atmosphere of rust, lifeless lead at its core, its oceans contending with the orbit of three moons."

"Fair enough," she says, "you're a sensitive guy. But this genre usually begins with a question and not a confession."

False Sermon—True Story

Like it or not, they get our weather tomorrow. Like us, they enter memory, assured it is finite. Tomorrow: winter in its one disguise. Tomorrow: a hitherto purely imagined form. You can toss, if you wish, salt in the fire as an offering. To be safe, you might as well throw in three rose seeds, three nettle seeds, two rue leaves, and three cumin seeds. Crushed cumin will not do. They call the secret poison *spider in the dumpling*. Write down the recipe in your little book of misfortunes, your little book of micrographia. The lacuna's deep taproot (which must not be pulled, but dug up), smells like a beet or a parsnip—sweet and loamy. It is to the tongue what the incantation of a broom is to the ear. Tomorrow. But not before the daily demise of evening. Each brushstroke had a name—*little hatchet, combed-out hemp, serpent's tail, the pulled carpenter's nail*—but they called it *spilled ink*, and went to fetch a mop. All the while forgetting the emptiness that is the site of transformation, the emptiness that is an intermediary. They waste a good deal of time waiting for intuition to flash forth, then fall prey to gloom. They could have called us. The wintery mix arrived here yesterday.

The Unexpected Returns

Despite our best efforts, we gave up renaming the constellations, given the confines of speech, nine always turning out to be six, the effort interrupted again by a motion to quash subpoena.

Night spread wide across the island until a dispersing agent spilled from a crop-duster. Then it was morning again with unexpected media coverage and roadwork ahead.

It seemed we had crossed an international dateline. All the color in the white angel's trumpet blossoms shivered as *white*. The moon covered the sun, as most are acutely aware.

Sometimes an image arises out of nowhere and its source (an old newsreel? a dream?) escapes us: a group of explorers look down where the ice thins; the sled dogs, agitated, bark.

The recollection, however, offers an unexpected return. It seems possible to retranslate the prophecy to benefit not just the rich, possible to draw the complexity of the ostrich plume's ginger as a single continuous line.

By Another Route

One is haunted. Haunted, one must proceed nonetheless with the courtesy of a host. One assumes the ghost is lost and needs to be helped on its way. One sees things others do not see. Or rather one sees things that others cannot see.

One surrenders. Gives in. Is overtaken. Possessed. One learns a new language that one speaks, as one reads, silently. Words given shape in the throat and mouth but not sounded. The experience leaves one short of breath, if not breathless.

How deeply a ghost hungers. It cannot eat. If it could, it would never be sated. Exiled as it is from the past and the future, a ghost resides in the here and now. The hour slows. Hardens. As translucent as amber.

: :

The difference between this world and the next is slight, barely noticeable, what one might call *a flaw in continuity* or *a bad splice.* There: the wheeze of a concertina. Here: a drain coming unstuck. One crosses a threshold uninvited. One, invitation in hand, knocks at the door ajar.

The *uncanny*, Freud says, is *something which ought to have remained hidden but has come to light.* One can recall the view from the palmist's window: dim, featureless, but not the fortune read aloud from one's own hand. The gaze is always introspective: dim and featureless.

Look: the grubby dun of a penumbral nocturne. One descends in the dark to the cellar to find the fuse box. Another worn set of concrete stairs, it seems, around each corner to take one deeper down in the mountain into which the cellar is dug.

: :

One subtracts everything that is not God and finds a minus sign. One returns to the dog-eared pages and finds little of significance. The marginalia, although cryptic, is in no way noteworthy or evocative. To find one's way, keep the mountain to the right.

Subtracted from the inventory: three thousand hand-carved ivory beads in a Cro-Magnon grave, a sieve to separate out prime numbers, the parabolic path of Holofernes' blood-splatter away from Judith's blade, Heisenberg's *formal description of the relations among perception …*

If sacrifice is necessary, Ai Weiwei says, *it must be accompanied by the appropriate ceremonies, as an unceremonious sacrifice is a crime against the natural world.* One removes layer after layer of the shellac's sulfurous yellow. Nonetheless, the painted mountain looks like a dung heap steaming.

: :

The ladder's shadow, more solid than the ladder, holds up the wall. Although the days grow longer, it gets dark early these days. The expected terminus never arrives. The wall leans a little now. One can hear at the base of the falls the water mend its breakage.

Dust alights evenly: a seamless transition. No skirmishes, no scrimmages, no play on words in a room with a single chair and a sign on the door saying: *Space for forgetting.* Here various pasts overlap. A line contains infinite points yet reads as an incomplete sentence.

There is nothing with which the night won't merge: conditional probability, pared-back harmonic distortions, or the vexations of a chance encounter. One can dowse for a single point of light, but find instead latent notions and primal forms. How strange, how other a body.

: :

Objects with an unobstructed line of sight with one another are said to be intervisible. One builds a house with sticks. Light and ocean seep through seams and cracks. Sea levels rise. The weight of the land sinks. Nonetheless, the view is uninterrupted.

In Bruegel's "Triumph of Death," a rickety wagon full of skulls passes. Two ships sink in the offing. Death on a reddish horse hauls an oversized scythe into war. In the lower right-hand corner, somehow oblivious to the battle, a lutist serenades his beloved.

As in the lightproof box of a camera, or in the depth of a cave, one finds a dark that transcends the absence of light, a dark virtually impenetrable, a dark that warps like an opaque plasma or malleable metal to touch. Then the shutter opens.

: :

In a dream, a yellow snake insinuates itself beneath the foot-worn marble stoop. Each flick of its tongue causes feedback and interference on the kitchen radio. When one pries up the stoop with a crowbar, the snake refuses to budge. Coils tighter.

A mere touch is enough to shimmer a plumb line. A serpent sheds its skin, but a serpent does not emerge—rather a sensation. The sensation of a thought. To liberate the unknown, one exchanges intention for chance. The day, hinged like a book, blows shut in a bluster.

One breathes in and the house fills. When the house is asleep what does the attic dream? A spell loses at last its adhesiveness thus must be spoken again. One breathes in and the house fills. When one breathes out how does the house not collapse?

: :

One comes burdened with maps, almanacs, and field guides. The source of the river is an underworld spring. To drink from it is to drowse, to forget the difference between cause and effect and happenstance, between yesterday and a series of irrational permutations.

(The repose of sleep refreshes only the body, Bachelard says. *It rarely sets the soul at rest. The repose of the night does not belong to us. It is not the possession of our being. Sleep opens within us an inn for phantoms. In the morning, we must sweep out the shadows.)*

The stag at the river's edge waits with the ageless confidence of a god. It does not drink— instinct leads the herd to glacier-fed creeks and meadow ponds. One will not recall the errancy, but one recalls the thirst. Having tracked the herd this far, one gives into thirst.

: :

The snow, earthward, is blown high again. Winter rehearses its single line of dialogue. Who can deny the ease of forgetting, deny the barbed precisions of each crystalline flake? Hidden behind gray clouds: a ruined weld of stars.

In the presence of a camera, time hesitates. It's like that moment when the horse breaks into a gallop and one feels oneself untethered from gravity. One is not flying but falling. Call it *what one has known all along*. Call it *the theory of unsupported transit.*

Begin with a footnote. Misalign the syntax as spindrift residue, as what a body transcribes through space: an inherent ephemerality, the flux of a dance enacted, the fixed site of the veering. Begin again. Draw from life as if from memory.

: :

Looking out at the sea, one is far from home. One loses track of the truth, which has the substance of shadow, of a stain that blooms on a wetted surface. A horizontal line makes of emptiness a sky—gray hovers over gray—a record of incremental change.

One acknowledges the duration. One embellishes and mistakes the middle distance for the elsewhere of late afternoon. Looking out at sea, one is far from arresting the image, far from pinpointing the coordinates, far from completing the required reading.

One is far from home and just now beginning to appreciate the scribbled formula left up on the blackboard all semester; to appreciate the Romantic potential of the grid and the way it holds each element in place. Far from home, one loses track of the truth.

: :

One is on a treacherous errand and finds Achilles among the breathless dead. He tries to speak but cannot. His face is a mirror of the past: blurred and distressed. One registers winter's redundancy as the remainder of a remainder. One takes the rough path up and out.

The night leans in like a reader over a book. The reader's own shadow makes the words dim and barely legible. One is like such a reader, which is to say one is like the night. One settles into read just as the light begins its haggard retreat.

We are surrounded by curtains, Magritte says. *We only perceive the world behind a curtain of semblance. At the same time, an object needs to be covered in order to be recognized at all.* Yes, one can bribe the dead, sacrifice a bird or lamb, let the dead wet their tongues. Yet one has come empty-handed.

: :

With the best of intentions, one refuses to assuage a hankering. One habituates the out-of-sync background noise and hears, at last, a pulse. *Don't jinx it for me*, one begs, but a spell cast cannot be uncast, only countered by a different spell.

How easily the objects become arrangements of shapes, shadows, and lines. The weather goes about its unmaking. The librettist awaits a collaborator. Awaits the interval, the harmony. *Say uncle,* one is commanded, and one gives in, gives up, begs for mercy.

One limits the set of conventions, or limits the colors on the palette to, say, terra rosa, yellow ochre, and cobalt blue, and this, then, becomes the *form,* the *constraint,* within which and against which one works. As if by a spell, the objects reassert themselves as *objects.*

: :

How to hold in mind all that might be of use: the Nile's flood schedule, for instance, or how often to have the chimney swept? One keeps one's eye open. The river widens, stretches toward the sea. Smoke uncoils upward like a length of rope.

If we keep the eyes open, Goethe says, *in a totally dark place, a certain sense of privation is experienced. The organ is abandoned to itself; it retires into itself.* The soul is dormant—suspended and asleep. Retired into itself, the eye cannot behold the soul as image or afterimage.

One attempts to fix and chart the ocean, to evaporate seawater to catalog the mineral residue. One holds one's breath and goes under. One's eyes adjust. But how to hold one's breath long enough? How not to float back to the surface?

: :

Furtive, fragile, one awaits a meaningful coincidence. Charcoal vestiges of the under-drawing muddy the clarity of the lead white. It does not take long to lapse into narrative, for the pretext to shear off the text like an iceberg from a glacier. One waits for such a coincidence.

What remains of prior decisions: erased gestures, a fault line visible at the surface. To enact a mirage, one hangs a turmeric-stained square of silk in front of a square of stark, rough white cotton canvas. To enact a monsoon, one waits like everyone else for the rain to fall.

Astray, one continues. One confesses to nostalgia, to the weight of longing. But one is merely guilty of misremembering. One sets out in search for the miraculous but soon settles for trial and error. One had a plan but returns by another route.

From This Day Forward

It's hard to get there from here, what with the detours, and worse, the makeshift memorials and all the rubbernecking. Yet staying put has its cost. The moon—unerasable—stowed in the lake's depth, for example, must be hoisted up by ropes, and rehung nightly above oaks. Let's agree that the gyrfalcon's belled jess gives its prey a little edge, a sporting chance. Let's agree that by their attributes—a jar of ointment, an ax in the head—we recognize the saints.

The Hyenas

A pair of hyenas stood at the door, dressed not unlike missionaries: black pants, white button-down shirts, their backpacks a little too snug under their armpits.

One said—*We agree with John Cage; art should not be used as self-expression but as self-alteration.*

The other said—*Or consider what René Char said about why he became a writer: A bird's feather on my windowpane in winter and all at once there arose in my heart a battle of embers never to subside again.*

Before I could get a word in edgewise, the one said—quoting I think Gaston Bachelard—*If a poet looks through a microscope or a telescope, he always sees the same thing.*

I had to admit these were some smart hyenas. Yet each time they spoke, their hackles went up and whatever they said felt like a threat. Not to mention the snickering, the tee-hee-ing, the saliva matting their chin hairs.

I stood in the doorframe. I didn't want them entering. I had forgotten whether hyenas are scavengers or predators.

I really have to go—I said, but the one hyena put his paw between the screen and the jamb.

Okay—he said—*but before we go, remember what Horace said—Many brave men lived before Agamemnon; but all are overwhelmed in eternal night, unwept, unknown, because they lack a sacred poet.*

The other hyena, tugging his friend away by a backpack strap, attempting to ease the tension, said to me—*Perhaps you are just that sacred poet.*

A Slipknot as it Slips

Escape the body for a while. Escape from the tired flesh, from doorways and mirrors where shadows brood. Slip like a snake from your skin into an ever-new raw glare. Give in. Let the past and the eternal vie for significance. You are a blank page in a census book, the elegant straight line of a censor's cross-out, the senseless and the clandestine, a little frenzy of wind. Slip the snare of birth, the unruly moment of perception, the grids and systems of notation. Let others sleepwalk. You are weightless. For you, displaced, there is no theory of weightlessness. You are the transit and the transport, the unaccounted-for anomaly, the ordinary pleasure of a slipknot as it slips. If you still had hands, what friction, what fire you might rub up!

Romantic Landscape with the Garden of Gethsemane

Enrobed in shadows, the woods invite one to tarry.

If given an exploded view, one might behold unquantifiable dark matter, a graphite under-drawing bled through, the trees rearranged, composed, variants of the present site re-sited: a tangled screen of vine and tendrils, a distorted perspective to undermine the *reality* of the pictorial space.

The ostensible subject of the scene—look, Judas is one of the torchbearers among the authorities—is overwhelmed by the fall of moonlight on leaves, what looks like crisp crosshatchings of chalk.

One might note as well the menacing fecundity, the weedy hardiness upon the inhospitable soil.

The receding depths are more forest than copse; the ruched waterfall is a diffuse blur.

A startled stag turns toward the viewer.

The School Nurse

He could see the nurse outside, a last breath of smoke released before she returned to her station to find him again, his third stomachache this week, after months of stomachaches. She shook down the mercury and without a word, placed the thermometer under his tongue. Twin silver lidded glass canisters held tongue depressors and cotton-tipped sticks. Beyond the acrid trace of alcohol on the thermometer, he detected starch on the pillowcase, a waft of Pine-sol from the linoleum and sink, and the wiry scent of dried hairspray mixed, of course, with tobacco. When she smiled, a waxy bit of lipstick smudged the white of one front tooth. When she saw him stare, she turned to the mirror and wiped the tooth clean with a tissue. She straightened the folded white cardboard hat that designated her as a nurse. The boy worried he might die or get well and thus, their courtship, long unacknowledged as chivalry requires, would come, at last, to an end.

Study for a Ghost

The space is still. Not empty.

The space is still not empty.

The word for it close at hand

Yet out of reach. The space

Is still. Empty. No. Not yet.

: :

The wintry light fails to illumine each object, leaving some suspended, some waylaid, some spectral. My brother, long dead, occupies my dreams. Borrows money. Needs a lift. I owe him, he assures me. The unrounded, almost two-dimensional flames of the driftwood fire flare, hover, unattached. On the test, the blank was not meant to be filled in, thus the instruction, "Leave the blank blank."

: :

The ghost neither trips the wire,

Nor activates the motion sensor.

As a result, the camera captures no image.

: :

The room is henceforth of no consequence. The hour held within, neither receding nor advancing, is inert, and in this, is typical of such hours in such rooms. The room is empty. Or rather, the room is emptied except for an outdated calendar. The door is ajar. Or the door is about to open but facing the window I do not see the door. The walls of the room are rain. It is as though I am underwater, and each sound arrives amplified and distorted. I can aspire in the room to knowledge of nothing and be rewarded. One day remains un-X-ed on the calendar. The room, not spacious, holds the cold of palaces.

: :

The river runs fast with thaw.

The sky, heavy with constellations,

Slumps like a ceiling's wet plaster.

Time is, as always, beyond rescue.

: :

A ghost is a guest offered little hospitality. The consistency of melted wax, a ghost is more a liquid than a gas, more an unsteady focal point than the distant sound of a lute being tuned, or dry snow spun up by wind into a fugue. A ghost is an object around which time does not congeal. Yet to *haunt* is *to frequent*, even if infrequently. The brief span of a waltz in an abandoned dance hall is not enough to call forth a ghost. A ghost does not betray a trace of itself in a mirror's shallow depth. A ghost, like a cloud, is not weightless, but no brass counterweights in the felt-lined case can balance the scale on which it is measured.

The Landscape in Theory: *A Meditation*

i.

One has been given a detached view: the mismatched edges of faded pinks and greens arranged in, or, rather, as a coherent composition. Yet to call it a *vista* suggests one would care to look: a scruffy edgeland, interrupted by the curve of an off-ramp; a factory downwind from a reservoir; industrial parks and warehouses; the quarry filling with inky water. Occupied space gives way to empty ground. The road peters out, it appears, into a schism of woods. Of course, the land is bound by one's apprehension: the field of view aligned with a visual field. One feels, nonetheless, as if one has been blinkered, numbed by the artifice of perspective, the fiddly details, the convention of a consistent vantage point. The place, although mapped, is stranded: remote, unverifiable, an appendix tacked on like some final reading of a parable, or, like an agenda yet to be determined, an afterthought after all.

: :

The border, however tenuous—a brink of sunlight between two showers—must be imagined by each who crosses. What is to be found there? The crossed hands of the betrothed? A horned spirit extorting tolls at the crossroads? No. A sawhorse someone sawed in half. In the chain link, memorial crosses braided from roadside witch grass.

: :

How does one distill from the ineffable an intoxicating yet subtle perfume? There are traces of fault left, test patterns and barcodes, a boreal birch forest buried by lava. Memory is like a fog nothing can scuff or sever. From a screen of static interference, the light fails, and the dark reemerges. History begins again between two rivers.

The context is withheld or held within: the categories muddied, the slippages slipperier. Was it snow hung in the plum's branches? Or the sticky silk tents of caterpillars? New accounting systems are put in place. A distinct knot is tied to tally each tide.

: :

One must exit at the last exit, trust a bridge suspended on echoes. The smallest species of whitetail deer live in the pineland of the Keys. Beyond the mangrove's prop-roots: a coral and sea grass wilderness. Listen—an instrument to mimic the sound of rain. Or perhaps it is the rain.

: :

Above rough coral bones, clouds open. Objects are farther than they seem. The light bends and what is beyond the horizon is somehow visible, a mirage: the light elusive, ever-changing, and yet one expects of it fidelity.

: :

The new development, the figment of it, is stilled, as if one had suddenly exited or were about to arrive. The schematic rendered in dull blue pencil overlays a composite: aerial views taken from different altitudes. The actual site itself has not been determined. The look of *nowhere in particular*, or *here*, but *here sometime in the near future* is the look aspired to. Ridges appear as depressions. A basin inverts to a mound above the grade. The landfill, filled, will be planted with native trees. Roads will divide and connect the monochrome lots. Shadows will root objects to the ground. The distance will be kept just as one keeps one's distance from it.

: :

Wilderness, that mercy of something vast, takes over the arable land. To discern the thicket's order, subtract, now, the dimension of time. Leaves and vines, in place of language, emerge from a mouth. Endless loops and exhalations, split seconds and measured hours reanimate desire.

: :

The midsummer sun all evening at eye level. A white enamel bucket by a partly opened door. Wind in the cow parsley. A stack of old floorboards pried up. A jar of nails. The moment is weather-driven, yet no rain falls to fill a bog cut. How easily a photograph hoards all one merely glimpsed. At the holy well: a fleeting glance of far away, the water's bell tone on limestone.

: :

Stray bits of thought. No legend. No grid of longitude and latitude to attenuate this unattended landscape.

: :

Above the Shannon, the starlings' evening murmurations, a pure medium like mercury, all transcience and transmutation, continue to torque and agitate as a twisted cylinder, as acute curves. There is no surface to see beneath, only a malleable density and depth, a flailed flail, an unwound winding sheet. Involved and involuted. Volatile.

ii.

Surf thuds deep in a wave-hacked cave. White half-moon fossils imprint gray limestone. Gulls taunt and chuckle. Sightings are taken for accurate alignment. The sun, as it does, stalls at noon. Interstitial fauna of marine sands shift. Wind recalls its antecedent as the world arranges as rhyme. Blackberries, bilberries, rowan, and sloes.

: :

Rising sea levels nudge the glacial till bluff landward. High up: mare's tails, parallel contrails diminishing against a scratched sky as opaque as cobalt sea glass. Sea level rise nudges the four hundred-million-year-old stones landward toward the salt marsh and lagoon they shelter. With each wave the cobbled beach clatters. The shifted stones lift and shuffle.

: :

Blue shadow on a Provençal hillside. A worker with two walkie-talkies in his hands shouts across the distance to his co-workers. Emerald glints on a pigeon's breast. Another worker, walkie-talkie in hand, shouts back. As in Ruskin's "Sepia Sketch of Leafage," light ambers the vine's full green.

: :

In the given world, beyond the ellipses, one notes the corollary of pond ripples and planetary orbits, the compression and release that is *motion*, the time-lapsed dispersion of a storm front as the menacing clouds unfold into a tracery of mists. One lives at the edge of the world, although it feels like the center.

: :

The auroras are an unstable spectacle, collapsing even as they rise, like a sinking ship buoyant on air water quickly displaces, an elaborate wreckage lost as the surface heals over. Flames shiver between opacity and transparence, static-abraded, effaced, then translucent, solid, seen-through as one sees through the Milky Way, a congealed mass of light, a hive of hollows held together by geometry. The insubstantial pageant—a baroque turbulence of randomly initiated ratios, a diaphanous lightness like water ripples preserved over time in stone—cools from rose to green, apart and parting, gaps in torn curtains, asymmetrical intervals hung as virga, as falls, as sheerness without edge or chasm, and is reabsorbed back into the black cold, into the icy scald and sear, a congealed glaze that snuffs and smothers any light that might try to escape it.

: :

Depth is conjured by way of elaborate angles on a Hindu miniature's flat two-dimensional space. No shadows cast. No highlights. Bent beside a stream, the god tastes the stylized water: the blue of his hands and face the blue of the cool clear river. Walls far and close in focus. All that is continues. Does not recede. Does not move. The epic length of a day beheld in a single glance.

: :

Obscured as one might say of light-fall. Or a distance haze hides. Each note is held, but at a whisper, as when dancers take the stage, and the curtain opens, and it is not yet the first day of creation.

: :

The *white* of the magnolia. A repertoire of rusted objects. The celestial bodies' calibrated but unseen influence upon one's fate. The ocean lighter than the sky. The eighteen flame-like points of the staghorn sumac. Sunrise through acidic humidity. Space compressed through a concave lens. An arrow-pierced saint tied to a tree. A sketch of a fletched shaft, of the tree alone without the saint.

: :

The way home—overlapping trajectories—resembles some archaic cursive used only for the holiest of texts.

: :

A few days remain nailed up on the calendar. Where the plot diverges one misconstrues a turn toward closure. The vast map of the frontier is refolded. One ignores the gaps in the taxonomy and is moved neither toward improvisation nor reiteration. All one ever has is a partial view, a view *on-the-cusp-of*, a view *not-yet-transfigured.* Like drizzle beheld from afar, a cloud appears to descend.

iii.

The dark closes in. The moon emerges, enlarges the *out-there* into a ghostly space without dimenision. The book of the night sky is redacted, charred like a burnt field, reduced to carbon. In the window—adrift, detached, disorienting—an oasis of reflection.

: :

Inside, a mirror hangs at an odd angle to its reflection, undermines the plumb and the level. The window overlooks a gibbous moon in a leafless willow. Each object is dusted with the residue of cast shadows, with the *once-was*, the arcane. Keats says he is *content to look on the mists of idleness*. Autumn is the longest season, albeit blurred and crepuscular. *In the midst of idleness* is how one misremembers it.

: :

The autumn sky, after all, fills in the space between branches, expands as the mass and volume of leaves decrease. One turns the hourglass over, but cannot restart time. A little dune accumulates beneath the cinch. There is little left to say about the anomolies of visual experience and the elegant austeries of understatement. One rolls the trashbins curbside weekly and by some miracle the offering is accepted.

: :

The dull, overcast-ness of the day registers as *mute*. The wood's edge obscures the view, if it is not itself the view. And if so, how quickly evening gathers like weather beyond the line of oaks. The picture plane's narrow limitations give way to an illusion of depth, an *into* that just might be entered, and entered—the air flecked with moss spores and leaf dust—surrendered to, a shade absorbed into shade.

: :

Stark, low winter light. The creek rough with thaw. The day moon is to the eye what an echo is to the ear. A scaffold holds up a single cloud.

: :

One is offered a glimpse, a narrow slice of landscape framed in the instant before the train doors close. The roads and paths lost beneath snow. Around one, the murmur continues as if conversation exercises culled and dutifully repeated from an out-of-print textbook. And when the train next stops and the doors open, the view is *another*, meaning at once *different* and *the same*, thus the unresolved tension, a feedback loop of damaged recovered data, is recurrent more than constant, its intended function exhausted. As if to recall a long-forgotten presence—some uncertain state between emerging and disappearing—one has set one's sights on what extends beyond the pictorial field. On the tip of one's tongue (meaning *what lingers just out of reach*), snippets of a folk song sung to see how, once circulated, it returns changed. Although the track is straight, one is asked to navigate by way of random coordinates, to feed the fire whatever burns. The embedded narrative is unacknowledged, yet one knows from experience the bridge is out ahead, the track ends snarled.

: :

One looks out to the slick slabs of coastal mud flats through a window's fragile filigree of ice and finds the low tide an alloy of pearl and mercury drawn taut in the offing. Or one looks up at stars and back in time and finds a chart to fix a point in space. One tests the limits of sight and finds limits, senses still all that is beyond the senses, has faith in an argument augmented by aught.

: :

In a clearing, one longs for the forest's depths, subdued blue hues of amnesia, but finds instead a past, a landscape salvaged from memory's wreckage. A ruined stone foundation tilts inward. The river continues to freeze and thaw. Surface ice shatters and cants, freezes once again to offer a jagged passage across.

: :

The borderline, a coast, constantly shifts. The destination is shadowed, hidden by the location marker.

: :

Beneath the inky wash of winter dusk: a snow-covered hedge maze. To see even this much, one must extend the exposure so that highlights amass on the surface of a dark shallow bas-relief. A path is all that remains of the passage.

iv.

A low horizon line cleaves the shallow space. One awaits the triumph of Pan as one story is grafted onto another. The delight of repetition modulates easily into the horror of repetition. The sky glows as neither dusk nor dawn. The bouquets in the foreground have been traced from a naturalist's miscellany. The central tree is charred, scarred by fires that never quite caught. Buried like a grub, the past mutates.

: :

One draws on memory but the flimsy surface tears. One enters the fold through the stile of a *therefore*. Therefore, a river is an errant arrow to the oxbow. As rational as a cloud, one settles for a tentative equilibrium. The river quivers in the wind, in the unquiet light. Only the scale changes: quarry scalpings, field stones, erratics …

: :

Presence annuls absence and, like memory, is incomplete. How rare for the eye to rest *here* and not on the view beyond: the wash of soot where nothing quickens, or disturbs the wet, dark membrane of loam that is this turned field.

: :

Sediment accrues and shifts. A tree fledged with jarring grackles empties. The afterimage fades on one's retina: an adagio afloat on a moment of pause. How otherworldly the rescued refugees swaddled in their silver foil emergency blankets.

: :

Without key or grammar, one understands the balance and impermanence of the dry stone wall. The break in its length, experienced as a *gate*, opens onto fields and beyond: slow sinuous lines of other distant stone walls, roof angles, sun-bright panes, an overgrown cherry orchard. One places a hand on the stone and expects to feel a reservoir of night's cold and mineral damp, but already the stone has absorbed the morning sun's heat.

: :

A forty-degree angle is formed by rain and the roof's incline. One does not hear the web tear but looks up at that instant and sees the web torn. Steam lifts from the iron. A window fogs. In the garden, a child traces with her finger the curves of reflected distortion upon a gazing ball.

: :

More often than not, one must break a trail into the depth of trees, part the dark as one might dig up a black slab from a bog. One stumbles in the midst of the scathed forest; regrets having entered the dense thicket lit only by a filament of light that is one's own body aglow.

: :

Streams. Runs. Kills. A ramble of runoff. Beyond or behind—a geometry of *neither nor* or *either or*.

: :

The stream pools then accelerates as it slopes toward the falls, beyond which a hazy horizon merges a tree line with sky. Power lines drape across the expanse. Time is embedded in the layers the moving water excavates. Two birdsongs overlap. Harmony like happiness is transient.

: :

The irrefutable changes day to day. With only tides to tell time, the standardization of minute increments is a near impossible task. Once measured, the hours in between become distance, the distance a scaled map. The tide stalls before it turns. The length of that stall is a single unit. Day to day the irrefutable changes.

Eurydice

We see her in the moment of her vanishing. She is there, then not. Of course, she has no agency. He turns. He turns back. And we see her. Gone. Vanished in a moment. And without agency. He turns and, because of his turning, she is swept back into the dark. Vanished, she is not there. Was she ever? Even for a moment? He turns, surprised to find her not there. The story would not be a story without that turn. Without her lack of agency. He turns in the dark and watches her vanish. Or, as he, the poet, would put it:

She slips away—a frail shadow at a threshold over whelmed

By lightning: banished, cast out, as quick as viper's venom—

No One Treats You Like a Mother When Your Mother is Dead

Seven or eight blossoms

On the little apple tree.

Barely a pie in the offing.

Only yesterday, my mother was a fifth grader bareback upon a donkey in Arkansas. Her house has a coal chute and a laundry chute: gravity the technology of the day. If she leans too far to pick a buttercup, she might fall off the donkey. The name of the donkey? Whatever she calls it, it responds. Already in spring, she thinks of autumn. There's the memory of the sound of sparrow wings in a hedge. Water in the creek working around rocks. Her father, his right eye a little clouded, dimmer than the left, is a widower. A widower in a town of widows, but he will not re-marry. She calls him Floyd, which is his given name. The past, unlike the future, is surround by a narrow margin of silence. The future is accompanied as always with sparse, plaintive music, as if to announce *something is about to happen*. The *something* unclear until it happens. A little dust whirls up, then disappears like a bit of advice from a soothsayer. *Lux. Lumina.* Wavelengths are absorbed or reflected. A thunderstorm interrupts the afternoon. Late summer, her garden thrives, begun with bargained-for cuttings from this widow or that. She likes the shadows cast by the lace curtains onto the pale of the pine kitchen floor. Someday, she thinks, I'll write it all down—not to remember, but so as not to forget.

Recently Recovered Pages from
The Complete List of Everything

A stand of birches. A clutter of grave goods. The compensation of levity. A theremin as a stand-in for birdsong. Pulleys and levers. Indigenous cannibals. Lightning's musket-flash. A wracked ship. A provocation or cure. A dumpster fire. The graphic notation of music. The end of enigma. Footfalls without echo. A backward glance. An untethered horse. A billboard advertising itself as a place to advertise. The prior state. An atlas of anatomy. River clay. A monument to entropy. The error introduced while editing a text. The past impinged upon by the present. A cigar box guitar. A do-over to re-do. The tents of the Red Cross. A hand-sewn fascicle. The endgame. A quarantine. Asemic writing. Gouges, mauls, and plummets. A punch line. An enslaved spirit. Mars black and lamp black. A complete list of everything (as of yet incomplete). The interior chamber of a camera obscura. Illicit trade and trafficking. A remix of the original. An argument in favor of the use of anachronisms. A caustic solution of lye water. That old narrative of katabasis and anabasis. The frosty white face of a nuthatch. A cello's scroll. Hand tools. Disambiguation. A bolete, a puffball, and a stinkhorn. The blue gills of a white cap mushroom. Straw spun to gold. A foil. An enemy. Either end of the continuum. The treachery of images. Albacore, alewife, alligator gar. The omen of a partial solar eclipse. The live version of Joy Division's "Transmission." A postcard from Barcelona. Ancillary work. A clear-cut ridge. The beautiful bird revealing the unknown to a pair of lovers. The nostalgia of the reactionary. Lead crystal. A benevolent coven. The killing fields. The killing floor. The killdeer. Every interplay of light and shade. Snakefruit. Soursop. Mouse melon. A trick of the eye. The phenomenology of dust. A slightly forced perspective. Eminent domain. An arrowless quiver. The interval in between. Windborne seeds. A rift. The affront of a taboo. The rabbit as trickster. A bonefolder. An egg balanced on an anvil. A bat-eared fox. A black lemur. A bush dog. A foothold on the rung. A fugue for woodwinds. Kiln. Crucible. Cauldron. Yucca fibers. A crisp. A cobbler. A pie. An unauthorized biography. Hair loose from a braid. Memory submerged in water. An open wound. Debunked conspiracy theories. Cloud chamber. Chamber music. Andirons (also called firedogs). Noun meaning *one who is highly sensitive to clichés*. Ill-intentioned ghosts. Random access memory. The improbable. The Industrial Revolution. Sludge build-up. A river silted in. An insinuated preamble. *Objets d'art*. Star anise. A naïve melody. A doomsday malaise. Newfangledness. Figure 63. Blind Willie Johnson's scratchy recording of "I Just Can't Keep from Crying." A flock of clothespins perched on the line. A foxglove. A shark's eye. Illegible inscription. A dream's function. A Clovis point. The tabled motion. A bog as a site to conceal a crime. Evaded taxes. An ocean trench. Basalt, granite, and rhyolite. A lute out of tune. More of a snag than a glitch. The Gospel according to Mary. Stolen passport. Calligraphic brushstrokes. Terra incognita. A smoke ring. The structure of an event. Cold Mountain. The unsent letter. The night watch. A thorn thicket. The *the*. Sleet. A marooned polar bear adrift on ice. The grinding pace of light years.

The River Still Ragged with Ice Floes

The woodcutter opened the wolf's belly with a well-honed axe, but found no grandmother, no girl, and no home-baked goodies. The wolf moaned, "Why did you gut me so? I told you that you would find nothing." The woodcutter filled the hollowed beast with gravel and stone, and sewed the wound shut with a tangle of fishing line. Before pushing the creature into the river still ragged with ice floes, the woodcutter asked, "Given the chance, might you have devoured a child, her grandma, and a basket of tasty treats?" The wolf, before it sank, replied, "I admit I am a wolf."

Buried for Now

An island is a body surround by water; a peninsula is something quite different, as is an inlet or isthmus; that said, the noontime objects hid their shadows; spoons in the drawer slept the sleep of spoons; I cannot remember the words or the silences, but have a vague recollection of the weather that linked them, floods and fallen facades; the answers came too easily, you said, as if someone were feeding me my lines from backstage; how long the smoke hung after rain, the bonfire smoke, the bonfire of ladders; even now, the fugue ache, the seven curses that turned back seven winds; the years continue to float on their sides like blue gill; your death certificate remains under a pile of papers on my desk, buried for now, easily exhumed; the stationary ran out, so I wrote on the motel room wall with chalk; the chalk ran out, so I wrote with water on the carpet; I did not bother to turn into the spin, my face in the rearview an apt self-portrait as the ditch approached; I was not a good son; the willow lashes at the wind, the wind lashes back; the exchange is untenable, is wreckage, is fraught, is over for now; an island is a body surrounded by water, a peninsula is something quite different, as is an inlet or isthmus; that said, I was not a good brother.

The Boredom that Precedes the Rapture

Stripped of ritual, your gathering takes on the mood of a dinner party at which you are neither guest nor host. Stewed turnips weep into the mashed potatoes. The cod is undercooked. You are about to speak your mind, but the words shimmy and dangle before your eyes like three or four wasps inside a revival tent. The woman next to you complains of a feather lodged in her heart. Her husband argues that memory, like an echo, diminishes over distance. You notice the pencil lines on the wall, which once marked their child's changing height, have been painted over. Outside: blue nocturnal shadows, red twiggy remains of shrubs above snow. With each click of the View-Master, the scene changes: the dining room displaced by a thicket of whispers. By hearsay. By heresy.

Lilith

after Kiki Smith

Upside down, spider-like on the wall, she looks up at us and meets our eyes. Her beauty, an unintended consequence, terrifies. Neither echo nor shadow. Singular. There is for her, in leaving no trace, no path of return. The fog lingers. The fog dissipates. Distance is brought close: the still riverbend, the web dew-jeweled. The present continuous, persistent, is *present.* She has no patience for that which comes after, for the belated. She sees us as we are: replicas. Creatures of darkness, distilled from light's residue: shovelfuls of soot and grit suspended in sluggish, waxy tallow.

The Weight

I pulled into Nazareth, was feelin' about half past dead

—The Band

He does not notice its dead, leaden weight until he has time on his hands. A single second is heavier than a sack of flour. He would need a car jack to budge a half an hour an inch off the floor. At night in bed, he cannot breathe. The hours stack one by one like stones upon his chest.

The Spectrum's Violet End

How little is required to obtain an illusion: minor adjustments to steer attention. You look through light, dust, and air—a plasma of sorts—to see the *thing-seen*, and yet the ragged edge of digital debris will not resolve.

Like an echo repeated on a loop, it quivers and oscillates: a thread snagged from a dream. A sense of trickery permeates.

You are plagued by the persistent recurrence of a visual image after the stimulus has been removed. The most common healing practice is touch.

Nevertheless, you are left thumb-worn as each moment is restaged with disquieting accuracy and an entire spectrum must be once again intuited from a black and white snapshot. You live here outside the mercurial borders without which there would be no trespass, nothing to forgive. Entangled in the everyday, you take down the strip of caution tape from the doorframe and enter again a place transformed. You do not and will not address the hypothetical.

Your mind is elsewhere: the painted background of mis-en-scene, an ever-widening range of countless grays and blacks on a fiberboard substrate. You keep forgetting the subgenre of the cumulative tales, the myth of specific gravity.

Roots upheave a concrete slab. Forms recur indifferently in the archival footage of the hinterlands.

As frequently as the wind, the magnetic poles switch orientation. Did you believe somehow that a sensation could be consistent *and* sustainable, could be recollected *and* reassembled, experienced again, not as a rhyme of the previous sensation but as the clone of the first sensation, its same self?

The flood, illuminated by the floodlight, looks like a wide plain of needle ice, a ragged passage over a thousand broken magic lantern slides. You are on another mistaken quest for God, ill equipped and ill at ease with the immediacy of the present tense.

You spend all night in the library bent over the card catalog. A few grains of discernible light adrift in the foyer. A transistor radio in the stacks, volume low, tuned to 1971. You have forgotten the astrolabe's function, have abandoned the grid, the increments, and units of measurement, the offered and opened hand, the breadth and length, even, of the here and now.

The past darkens like fog-murk toward the spectrum's violet end. Cloaked in a drab camouflage that neither hides nor mimics—tomorrow stalls ahead. All the clocks have stopped. How to recalibrate the gears, to recalculate the pendulum's weight and arc?

Border Crossing

The conspiracy theory spreads as a virus. The same old same old: spectral figures in a liminal space, the characteristic vacancy of a vacant lot. Wind turns the weathercock. There, on the cusp of logic, we call the crows with a clap and chart chance. Horses cross from the island at low tide. A cloud where the island should be. A whole cloud in a tide pool. Falling flowers hide the figure of Krishna. We brought the wrong map but follow it, nevertheless. Brought along the wheel, the lever, and the screw. At the border, the customs official is hungry for English conversation, but speaks only in incomplete sentences:

A cornfield north of Clear Lake, Iowa

A ruckus in the rookery

Chet Baker singing "My Funny Valentine"

How disappointing, we concurred, upon finally hearing it, is the nightingale's song.

Oblique Strategies

A motionless nimbus, isolated from the cloud-cluster, suspends above my head. Whatever happens before a camera is a performance: Jupiter dwarfed by the moon, for instance, or the door not ajar but lifted off its hinges. The crows gyre up all at once. As vulnerable as one is in a trance, I am caught in the wake of my own displacement. I find as a workaround a shallow flight of stairs, a vignette (*as from a vine*). Like a sleepwalker, I await an echo or reverb, for waves to break their silence.

The Sick Boy

The child is about to wake or about to give into sleep. The time of sickness passes like a dense current of fog that moves around him as he stands still, or parts uneasily as he steps into and through it. The fog is like a snowstorm, a whiteout, but not cold. Moments of clarity break through. What to call them—visions? He is a child which means he is not whole, complete, finished, or singular. He is fragmented, split like a dropped vial of mercury. Atomized. He is the child nonetheless the heavenly host addresses, and he hears it when others cannot distinguish it from birdcall, wind in the attic, and radio waves. If seen by someone from a distance, the child imagines he would be out of focus, a blur, a figure not wholly solid, like a ghost or cloud wisp. A near-sighted boy, that is how he sees distant things—lights haloed, aflare, the edges of trees smudged against the sky, the sky grainy. Translucent. Dispersed. He wants to be well. Returned to school and the hurry of the day. At school he is known as *the sick boy*. Hand-drawn cards encourage him to *get well soon*. He has been sick for as long as he can remember. Yet what can he remember? One day a new refrigerator arrives, and he is allowed to spend the entire day inside its abandoned cardboard box, which he imagines a space station, a jail house, a bunker. But the next day it is folded up curbside with the rest of the trash. This is still years before the moon landing, the riots, the city an underlit dome of smoke in the distance. What is wrong with the child? That is what everyone is trying to figure out. Exploratory surgery is scheduled. They will open him and see, his mother says. In a new movie called *The Fantastic Voyage*, a miniature submarine with doctors and scientists on board enters a man's body by way of a syringe. His mother says they will open him and see. He imagines his insides out—unpacked, unraveled, fingered, scrutinized, held up to the light—only to be repacked and, if he had the word, he would hope not *haphazardly*. First, they will put him under, then open him and see.

Sonatina for Mark Strand

One arrives from the future to disrupt an event in the past. A side effect of time travel is that one arrives in the past with no memory of the future. Now, in the past, unaware of one's task, one watches, powerless to intervene, and the event occurs, as it must.

One arrives from the future to find that loops and skeins of roots entwine the reclining Buddha. There is a pause in the monsoon. Clouds are mended and re-torn. Having arrived from the future, one is hungry, naked, and of slender means.

One arrives from the future as if from a shoreless ocean, a darkened room, a circle formed by standing stones not original to the site. One arrives from the future, uninvited, as welcome as a beggar, as unnoticed. The past is always there—there in the distance—a thinning cloud of squid ink.

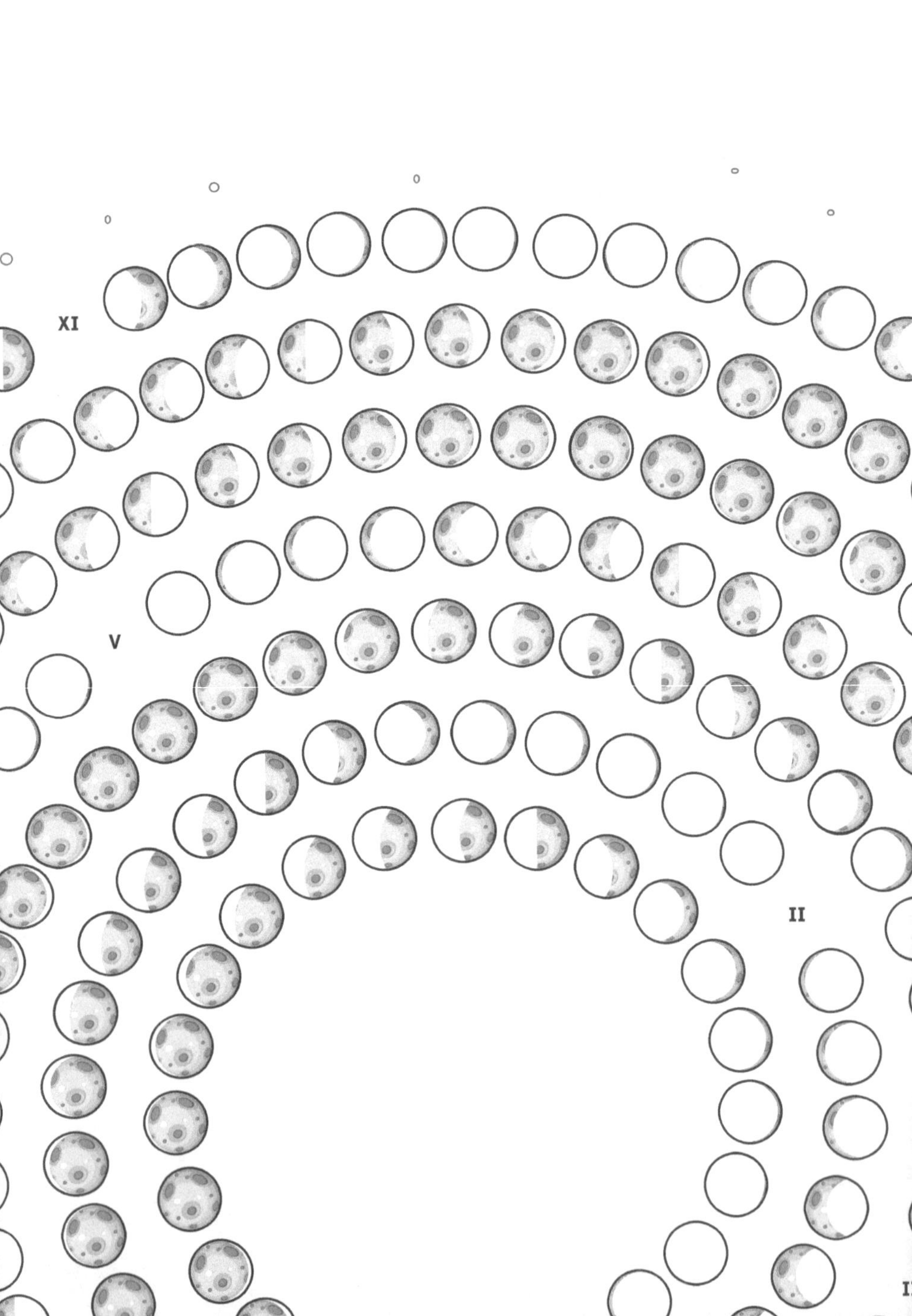
XI
V
II
I

II.

Katabasis

At the pace roots grow, I descend into the depths but with no exit plan. If there is a hell to harrow, so be it. If in digging, magma is released, and lava flows downward to the sea, so be it. If the shades will not be coaxed forward by sacrifice or bribe, so be it. Downward to darkness, like a drowned man with stones in his pockets.

: :

Was it night fears or fever that embodied me, burned a thousand scriptures onto my retina, that dull gray slate onto which things are written, incised, or engraved? Permanent yet somehow inaccessible? Stress determined the measure, the length of the possession, the night's uncharted expanse. Now I lay me down. Now and forever. My soul the size of a whisper, as quick as a whiplash, as the wings of what I hoped were angels sequestered in the periphery. Now I lay me down. Now.

: :

East of here: the night, noisy with a skulk of foxes. The past leaks through the present's porous membrane. A waterfall shapeshifts in and out of light: rush and spray, clash and overlap, reflection giving way to stone and moss. Can I shed my shame as a snake sheds its skin? A tree stump's new growth entwines the lodged axe head. I come prepared: a libation allows the dead to speak. A sugar cube on the palm tempts the horse nearer. A seeker, I close my eyes, count to ten, ready or not.

: :

I encode, encrypt to make secret intention, whether hex or spell, glyph or sigil: language spoken to speak the world into being, yet cloaked, shrouded, concealed, by its very name.

: :

I forget how much time has passed between acts or how in the next chapter a new generation will follow the same, seemingly fated, path of their forebearers. I forget the pleasure in pattern, in repetition. The morning is contained by the pace of the sun, a distance measured by the shrill of a jay's call. Sometimes words like *Amen* or *O* or *Hallelujah* sit unspoken, and I can taste them there on the tongue: a plum almost too ripe, the bitter of parsley, the flawlessness that is salt. A scent lingers. Perhaps burnt eucalyptus meant to clear the air? Other elusive remnants remain unidentified, like some ash darker than shadow, ash bees disperse from field to field after a battle, where the hero, distraught, descends into the underworld unguided, to consult the shades on some errant errand.

A Child Knows Exile

Forgotten on a department store escalator, a child has access to the noetic, has felt severed, disassociated, possessed by demons, abducted by aliens. A child knows vastation and glows like a filament in a bulb; blown out, rekindles like a trick candle. Forced from home daily, dispossessed, and told to sit quietly in rows, a child knows exile. A child makes a chain of clover, consults the company of clouds, invents the notion of an imaginary friend named Sandy Belinda, who all too often sasses and talks back. *Make a wish* the grownups insist. But the flame will not be quenched. No. The flame grows higher.

A Dithering of Presences

To petition for rain, one offers a fern pressed in a field guide of ferns, a thrum of bees in a hay meadow, the veneer of the real, the certainty of silence. One offers what is at hand, as this crisis or that punctuates the moment. As a word awaits its antonym, constellations tangle in a weft of time. The clothesline in wind is flung with ghosts. One is at the mercy of some agency—call it *ache*. Call it *desire*. One straps on ritual as if a yoke. How to braid an intricate rope of snakes? How to translate an inaudible vibration into a visible spectrum, into a stone sutra? At midwinter, one thirsts for light. The forced forsythia branch in a vase illuminates the darkened dining room. What awaits? A second chance? A late romance? How to map the unfolding of the starlings' murmuration?

The House

The room is in a house in a clearing, a house built from the trees cleared to make room for the house. The house a kind of exoskeleton. The cellar, ankle-deep in sludge and seepage, is cave-cold and compact. The attic conceals clues to the past, but it's too dark up there to pick the trunk's lock, to read the bundled letters, or the foreign postmarks.

Metamorphosis

The timeless moment, a caesura, unfolds in a fraught space: a field sick with poppies, a closeup of ferns as a stand-in for a forest. Confronted with a god's illogical will and urgent desire, what else but awe, terror, and dread? How often the victim is pictured as not panicked, but placid, willingly giving into the god, as if metamorphosis were not a rupture. Not this wreckage beyond salvage. Not a piercing. Not a plucking.

The Invention of the Camera Obscura

Where the arcs of two barn swallows intersect: make that the vanishing point. Where receding lines converge, where the temporal is suspended, where the ephemeral is condensed and lodged, place there, at the pinpoint, a lens cut and ground from a glacial core sample.

Watch how the image, projected, is inverted: the winter landscape, upside down, keenly in focus, white on white, a flawless blankness, a candor, a glare— (in response to which all gathered say—*O*—)

Interior with White Door

Light slants in from a high window: an axis at a tilt, a line around which the story's progress drags. Where to hoard stolen moments, the nothing-hidden of the still-unmade bed, the tedium and promiscuities, the infinite regress of a reflection's reflection? How not to feel like a patient who waits, ill and ill at ease, in the waiting room: impatient, embarrassed, undressed, cold, yet sweating?

File Not Found

As they disclose the gist of bioluminescence, fireflies eclipse the Milky Way. There's a smolder in the kindling. The inexhaustible alluvium, like holy sand at Chimayo, drifts, clogs the cogs. Nowadays, it's hard to learn much of anything given that each error is fatal. Remember *to forget* is not the opposite of *to remember.*

Pareidolia

—In dim light: a dim silhouette. Amid staticky noise: a signal.

—The object is resituated, defamiliarized. Distorted. Disfigured by context. A yellow quince, for instance, in an illustrated herbal.

—The moment lived twice is not experienced as *deja vu* but as a stutter, a stub.

—A taut single line. Plucked, it resonates a note that once heard, expands beyond the range of hearing.

—Volition or violation? What a comfort to ignore, to disregard the precarity of the present, rushing as it does into another tense, another tension.

—I sweep so that the dust can settle elsewhere. What overlays becomes in time entangled.

—The fault of a fishbone crack widens. Curves and volumes resolve as a nude.

—The surface seethes, verbs and reverbs, a touch like a torch, as time unfolds at various velocities.

—Like the subtitle's subtleties—neither translation nor paraphrase—the mask protects as it disguises.

—Close at hand, reflected in the river: star-fall—elusive, quicksilver—blossoms, is a blossoming, as intricate as a cat's cradle, as a loop of string contorted: *cratch-cradle, manger cradle, creche*—a loom that allows for and limits the weave's complexity.

—An enclosed garden. Autumn holds back winter for now. The sky is like tea steeped too long. Murky. Bitter.

—Observed, the observed becomes a fiction, an end which is a continuation. The forecast for the forest is disaster. The wound: site specific. Arrivals and departures will not be updated.

—Meaning accumulates secretly, shimmers away: salamander-like.

—On a salted breeze, the ragged edge of a fiddle tune. In woody debris, a cloister of snails.

—Arctic lichens scab the erratic. A nest of antlers someone's hoarded arranged in a circle. The smell of thaw: apricity's intimacy.

—Spawned from chaos: the *nothing-out-of-which*, the *empty*. As form gives into the vast of formlessness, particles collide, ricochet, spiral.

Walking Mike One Winter Day

Venus at its nearest to Earth. The sky is immense, glimpsing, as it does, all of time. The atmosphere encircles the lithosphere: a wheel within a wheel. If I wait for a thaw, the path will be impassable. The dog, ahead—a scout, a diviner—returns as if from a future to the past. Here, I long for the hereafter, not the hitherto-little-explored. I weave each day out of drift and focus the way currents weave the air out of so much distance, vapor, and dust. The dog moves on, nose down in the text of it all, the web of reiterations, and somehow snuffles up a shed snakeskin in sleety ice as I follow, as I long for an interior, a single space contained within limits.

The Door

The door swings open onto. Into. Closes out. Closes in. The door offers an illusion of privacy. The door is a lever. The hinge, its fulcrum, balances the weight. Plain or ornate, the door is sculptural. Unhinged, robbed of its function, the door is cumbersome, unwieldy. The future, against which the door is locked, is worn away—neither portal nor aperture. The door in the dream is merely *door*—shed of significance, of uncanniness.

Of the Epic One Recalls a Passage

The loom's rhythm lulls the suitors to sleep. One prefers the perfected proportions of nostalgia, the permanence of objects over object permanence. One is comforted by how the accident recurs until flawless. Not an accident at all. Of the vast, one knows fragments; of the epic, one recalls a passage through a swamp, an abandoned drawer used as a makeshift crib. One proceeds not by way of divination, but a to-do list. In the distance, a stark architecture of sunlit beehives, fallow fields sown with land mines. Autumn: an old dog gnaws at a burr. Hours pass but who recalls the backfilling of each minute?

A Torpid Heat Stirred a Little by Cicadas

Sleep is singular. Unshared. Fraught. In the dream, one has a feather with which to separate the sea, a Dixie cup of water with which to extinguish a burning stump at Old Man's Creek, a mirror behind which to hide one's nakedness. Night settles first in the cypresses. One pursues a horse (requisitioned in the war) over two gray winters; one is delayed on the minimal stage-set of a Venetian staircase. Like a squatter, a ghost—substanceless, incorporeal—occupies a wardrobe. This after all is just a whistle stop, she says with a scavenger's discernment. Night settles first in the cypresses, then fills in from the bottom up.

The Direction of the Journey

As narratives overlap, what is predicated upon what is the mystery. Wolf moon in a starless sky. The landscape redacted by snow. Superimposed upon the map, an arrow delineates the direction of the journey. As if to reinstate enchantment, one frees oneself from the urge to decipher meaning.

Backward to Zero

On the uncluttered levelness of a tabletop, a still life performs stillness. One falls into language. One fails at language. One feels one's way by way of words. Thought's structure branches, and like roots confronted by obstacles, contorts. The tension, contained, is called nightfall. To keep from levitating, one lies down in a circle of stones, counts backward to zero. With a radio as a medium, one communicates with the spirits of the dead. The rain's salutation repeats: a felted hammer upon a string. One longs for the weightless sleep of horses but is given instead a lapse of memory, a drained lake, a thaw of permafrost.

Errors in Continuity

Among things other things: fog to the gorge brim, an alignment of seasons, the constellation of notes one calls a variation, a backward glance, boreal mosses and lichens in swathes. How a ladder implies a story. The released arrow's whisper. The errors in continuity as time lapses or loops. My interests are conflicted and fitful. What if the *divine* is endless emptiness, or something less—an interval between stars? I am tired of living already in a hypothetical future, of the rock tumbler's rumble 24/7 in the detached garage, of the prophetic dream translated as always into mere words.

The Visitants

Eddies and rills translated into surface. Dizzying depths of stars above the bonfire entangled as embers do. We awaited the souls—the palpable spirits—but the destination as well as the starting point proved unstable: each thought mediated by memory, by what we have come to call memory. We had the narrow refuge of a sentence, a frayed instant fleeced with moss. Abstracted, the noise became a song, the fruiting body of some rhizomatic complexity. *To-be-without-intention*: beyond us as before.

Shadows seeped. Soon darkness soaked the ground. Nature—untouched—appeared ramshackle, thumb worn. We were a little too late for too little too late. The quest for everlasting life put on hold given the rent, the accumulating burden of intergenerational guilt. Ours was an ill-kept errand in the wilderness, a detour. The door caved in. Saplings broke through floorboards. Rain pinged in scattered pots. Tree frogs chirped, hidden against the floral jacquard of the mildewed, heavy draperies. The self after all was the theory of the self, jerry-rigged, as fragile as a cage of twigs used as a prop in a production of *The Magic Flute*.

All remained untallied, untabulated, and fell short. The shutter clicked a moment too late and failed to capture a minor gesture, a sincere effort toward mimesis. Still, we rummaged through the past as through a drawer of photographs, recognizing the mountain crag, the foreboding glacier edge but not the faces or occasion. How reassuring that all the answers are in the back of the book. A sea of clouds. The silence rubbed out. A turn to the present tense to confirm a coming to closure. We face forward, imagine the future there, unruly in its splendor: water healing over a capsized boat.

Remain Seated for the Duration

One's position is pinpointed on a grid of longitude and latitude, a net of contrails, a frozen, woven substrate. From above, the archipelago looks like a broken, scattered scythe blade. The clouds: fresco-like, dry, without reflection. False indigo and fool's gold on polished plaster. One remains seated for the remainder of the flight, having conceded to the solemnity of departure, to the imputability of arrival.

Local Habitation

The curve of the shoreline is cluttered this morning, noisy with a congregation of gulls. Holding up a crab's tangled remains, one child chases another. A pelican—large, ungainly—sits motionless like a statue on the plinth of a mooring post. A glitter of flies lifts from a fish head. Untidy chickens peck at each other, pick up the this and that they find to eat in the sand and tidal debris. A cock crows but marks no hour. The sun, hidden as it is in clouds, offers no clue. The other child, now, has claimed what's left of the crab, and the chase recommences. The gulls, startled, rise against the wind. A cargo ship disappears below the horizon and the horizon heals shut.

: :

The horseshoe crab scavenges, tolerates the high turbidity, shelters in the shallows and roots. The waves are paltry: water encroaches, water recedes in this rookery of brown pelican, belled kingfisher, egret, and heron. Light interleaves with shadow, shadow with reflection. Deep into the story, no plot emerges. A sudden rain. Water hurries and rills. The *now* (like a dream?) so easily forgotten.

: :

In the sudden glare, the indigo of distance retreats. I see not the out-there, but the inside of my own eye: floaters—specks and threads—drift across my vision as if something enlarged on a microscope slide: an entire undersea world on a thimble-wide curve of seeing. And with a blink, I refocus, and the mazy swarm of vitreous gel disappears and what I am looking at is what I was looking at: frigate birds riding high thermals. Circling. Strange. Archaic like pterodactyls.

: :

A spider lends thread to the wind, which streams, sunlit, aflare into invisibility. Green anoles freeze then dart, find a flaw in the mortar and disappear. The day completed in haste, unrevised. The salt grinds, wears the coral to grit and sand. Wind and waves: an unmuted motion. As glaciers formed, sea level dropped as much as a hundred meters. The exposed coral forests died and collapsed into these islands, now only a few thousand years old. *Again* rhymes with *the end. The end* with *again*. Reverse the process and sea level rise will soon enough subsume the islands.

A Tomb for Hart Crane

For the solitary ferry passenger, there is no destination, merely distance. The bow plows through black water, leaves a wake like a furrow, and the wake heals over over time.

: :

How to discern in the dark depth of the sea *up*, when light has been wholly diluted to its opposite?

Space Which is Said to be a Void

From an open door, one hears Little Willie John sing "You Give Me Fever." *Fever in the mornin', fever all through the night.* It must be 1958 and one is not yet born, but on the way. A seed, placed beneath the tongue, allows the singer to sing. The drawbridge remains drawn. Anchored at a starting point, one feels the moon's vague tug, the moon a little circle drawn with tailor's chalk. A cold gondola slips into ground fog. One's eyes are blanks with cataracts. The dream, wasp-paper thin, tears at any attempt at translation. Through an appliance store window, one can see five TVs in row as the same black and white staticky test pattern shimmers and glitches on each bulbous screen. Up close, one can hear the crackling of light emitted—the sound of the light—and one imagines all of space, which is said to be a void, scratched and entangled with that sound.

The Turquoise Trail

Around me, a little solitude. As in a Persian miniature, perspectival hierarchies flatten out into the map of a garden from which I can only be expelled. I long to fly but forget how thin the air gets up there. At the threshold of dusk: the smell of rain before it arrives, the luminosity of a reduced palette, distant desert blues, the notation of a single star, which is not a star at all but a residual artifact: time woven on a star-shaped loom.

River Ice

From a single window, a farmhouse sheds light onto the dark. Ice and snow level out the terrain. In that room, dust floats in the desk lamp's cone: a curve of constellations. The sky, a hinterland gray, covers a predawn, purplish bruise. Who are you? A lost ghost? An overexposed memory? Depression is a kind of exile. You have arrived. Or you are just leaving, the young man who kills himself and displaces the now and the next—the afterlife merely that: *after life*. Nevertheless, the hundred-year half-life of longing and shame ticks like river ice breaking up on the Missouri.

October in Key West

The work remains the same: to reconcile the remnants into a whole, to make of the past a place I can revisit. Yet, that for which I am nostalgic is not the past, but its ephemerality, an elusiveness never quite realized, never quite fully thwarted.

What is the difference between a still image and a moving image of that same still image? Is the weight of time upon each the same? Or do we sense the jittery transmission, the twenty-four frames per second as the heavy hand of form?

I need a reader, an intercessor to answer these and other questions piling up like the mail I forgot to stop before going out of town. Vacation? Work? It does not change the absence, the correspondence that goes unattended, the bills past due.

Never mind the turbulent clouds, the uncharted routes, or nameless destinations. The privacy provided by a folding screen is all I need at times like these, something to stand behind. Here, the banyan sends down prop roots, which intertwine, thicken, spread, as if a grove, outward indefinitely. But really, a folding screen will do.

Natura Morta (1952) Giorgio Morandi

Suffused by light, pervaded with silence, free from any complicating narrative dimension: the eloquent fixity of things, the still life as aphasia, a suspension of language, a calm of counterpoint and mathematics removed from fervency, infused with restraint, a spell of enigma, and disquieting mystery.

Each assembled object (a narrow range of muted tones) in the repertoire is impersonal, familiar, an ideal example of the *ideal.*

The Restoration of an Altarpiece

They believed the old myth: from a single empty point, complexity: a constellation of infinite connections: a spectral web: a thousand lenses through which to focus an image so briefly exposed it exceeds resistance: the measure of a conductive material's opposition to current flow: a small spark annotated: a reciprocity of beauty and terror: the elegance of a knot: a tree branch cut away and healed.

A Room in the Palace

You cannot access one room without passing through the previous rooms. You expected privacy for the price of the room? A place where you might sleep through the night uninterrupted? Others must pass through your room to get to their own. A dream-logic perhaps, but the reality of such lodgings. Sometimes a guest stops to chat, wonders where you got the extra pillows, or the exceptional reproduction of the same painting that hangs in their room, but theirs looks embarrassingly amateurish. There is no exit from the final room except back through the all the other rooms, and of course, that is the guest with whom you've become most familiar as she sleepwalks through your room each night.

Breezewood

In the motel room, you try not to imagine the previous lives that have filled the space, that have left yet remain, not to haunt exactly, but to crowd nonetheless the square footage. Turning the heater down, unmaking the bed when you go out for ice. With the curtains pulled wide, you can predict the weather, watch as rain walks the distant ridgeline. You behold yourself in the reflection's voids and absences. There's no place to store one's clothes, let alone the secrets kept, the promises broken. Here time passes like a long sermon. Here time scuffs, snags, and stalls. Congeals or coagulates.

Mr. and Mrs. Stevens

The couple seem to have absorbed one another. Or is it that they have successfully repelled each other? Each is mutually invisible, sensed only as a force, like gravity. Still, one cannot describe the pull, the attraction. Void of obvious emotion, they attend the estate agent's open house and find it open, try to imagine themselves in the space, a space staged with the accoutrements of a life: suggested but without the untidiness, the clutter. A place two ghosts might haunt. Each ghost, though, unaware of the other. Or aware but each certain there is no such thing as a ghost.

A Tomb for Wallace Stevens

The soul sleeps where the serpent sleeps, tucked amid a cache of leathery eggs, and hibernates through the cold—the seasons of cold, the eons of cold—and roused at last by some stirring in the nest—a bit of straw, say, nicked by a spark to blaze—the soul uncoils, tears the loose skin pouch that held it, and, as it speaks in sibilant tongues of flame, the hibernal distance begins to thaw, the Northern Lights dim and fade.

Aperture

A dancer, in the company of gravity—suspended, or falling—(how to distinguish in the moment?) accompanies gravity. Falls. An abstraction. An invitation. A transference. Pathos as a verb tense. The level air's contour disturbed. A dowsing. A substance of intervals. Awakened echoes. The dancer aware bodily of the unseen (an angel in the blind spot, the shadow of a raised hand, a mirror with no reflection). The light almost liquid as it wraps. As it warps. And in drowsy assent, the dancer falls.

Arcana

The solvent alters. The durable erodes and is transformed. A weathervane does not challenge but gives into the wind. Its function is to make visible the wind's will. The moon sheds jade: a held breath released.

: :

Two images set upon one another—the overlay of a double exposure—defy the time that distinguishes them. Matter's alchemical mutability calls for the suspension of disbelief. One sings a little song to summon the ancestors, whose faces are painted red, a red derived from insects that eat only prickly pears.

: :

When one gets close enough to see, the mirror fogs over. A constellation of small stitches. Mud flats submerged in brackish water. One speculates with a lack of knowledge. Ambivalence eludes categorization, the dull hum of the humdrum.

: :

The distance between a thing and its name: a maelstrom, a fictive space, an endless storm on Jupiter. What are one's poems about? About how one thinks in language, how language gets in the way of thinking. How one fails to acknowledge beauty: the uneasy scribbles like hesitation marks.

: :

An object displaced to a vitrine is renamed, recontextualized. Asked to reweave a spider's web, one constructs a tiny loom, spins dust and mist into thread. One works at a remove as if one's life were a novel. No, a novella. No, a short story.

: :

A ruin houses earlier ruins. Among these ruins, one tallies the ambiguities, their variety. One recounts the contrary pleasures of lighting and snuffing a candle. One brings a covered dish, asks to ride shotgun, complains about the tyranny of taxonomy.

: :

The room, empty, says little about the lodger displaced. Forgetting is, if nothing else, a filter, a barrier by which the onslaught is delayed. The holdall holds little. As if a weather balloon descended, a small gray cloud fills in the clearing.

A Mask Allows for Transformation

A basalt island juts up from the water, more tower than landfall. The dream is heavy with glacial silt. Raven chatter on the petroglyph beach. Ice drifting. Adrift. The kayak skids on rounded gravel. Strewn with mica: the night sky. A relic narrowing: the glacier retreats.

Like the Past

Light penetrates to the mossed, leaf-littered, and lichened forest floor. Out of the palpable silence, the baroque effusiveness of a cuckoo rises and dwindles. Then is answered. The story changes with each telling. That is how I recognize it as a story. Between the woodlands and river, a wide expanse of flooded stubble: vast, largely inaccessible like the past. Wool snagged on fences. Burrs snagged on wool. My words are my own, yet sound unfamiliar: secondhand, echoey, disembodied, as they are on the low, unstable frequency of *meanwhile*.

With Each Telling

A girl, to her surprise, walks on water. The story differs with each telling. On the Sabbath, a girl steps out onto the water and continues like Jesus in three of the four Gospels. One Sunday morning, a girl walks on water to save her drowning brother. The girl does not walk on water, of course, but on steppingstones just below the rain-swollen surface as she hurries to save her brother. Witnessing from a distance, church elders believe she is walking on water. She is accused of being a witch. That her brother drowns despite her ability to walk on water only confirms the act's malevolence. The walked-upon water is a vernal pond and by late October, just before the trial, has shrunken to the stony, boggy basin of a meadow. The girl is found guilty of being a witch and is killed. Details of the method of execution vary.

A Field of Crutches

What he has learned in school, he says, is an order by which to connect unrelated things. Asked his age, he takes the question as a challenge. Each night: a dream unresolved. Raised voices. Improbable distances. The moon a dismal tincture. When he prays, he says, his prayers spread before him like green fronds of ferns. He knows from reading the theosophical treatise *Thought-Forms* that the shape of *devoutness* is distinct from that of *devotion*. He can talk binaries and absolutes, has a theory on the hierarchy of senses, knows crocodiles forage opportunistically. He believes a simmering dread infects his classmates (he can sense it in their auras) as well as his teacher, who left over winter break a Miss Appelbaum (the named reminded the boy of his favorite food—applesauce with cinnamon) to returned married, called now, to all their dismay, Mrs. Crutchfield.

Keep Your Lamp Trimmed and Burning

After rain, a droplet trembles a little before it falls. His father says, Go out and play, as if handing down a condemnation. The hours spill and elongate. The boy sits a step above her on the stoop. When her brother comes out, they will all play mumblety-peg. When she bends forward to pluck at a weed, he can see her small pale breast through the armhole of her sleeveless blouse. Her brother, who wants to be a preacher, says, Jesus is coming. She pulls their three pocketknives from the damp earth, hands them back blade-first. The bushes are beset with bagworms. Jesus, her brother says, Comes like a thief in the night.

An Arrangement

My mother, drunk often, would (inexplicably to me) pick up the pace. She was sweet then. Loved the world. Would send me out, a boy of nine or ten on a bike to pick up a carton of cigarettes, a fifth of vodka. (She had an *arrangement* with Louie, the store manager.) And though three bottles were in her cupboard, she feared running out and thus, I pedaled back and forth. Louie shook his head as he bagged the bottle, saying, If I catch you drinking this, son, your mother is in big trouble. Yes, sir, I said, as if we were in a play and this my one line. To which he would reply, I'm serious, son.

Once, during an ice storm, her stockpile dwindled. She panicked and suggested I ride up anyway. Just in case the store was open.

Wouldn't it be good to get out of the house, she said, and away from your silly mother?

The Lovers

The lovers do their job. Each invents the other. Holds and channels memory. The body of memory. The body as memory. Each like the moon gives back light. Each a voluptuary. The *is* and *always* of imminence.

Enthusiasms

I admit to enthusiasms, to earnestness, to ecstasy. I love you with a hollyhock's candid nakedness. I love you with the extravagant complexity of tree roots hidden from view, with the ease of a creek snaking through marl and marsh grass. What is the algorithm for rain-falling-on-a-mountain? Why are dreams so harrowing, yet delible? Forgotten? As Pablo Neruda says, *I love you without knowing how*. A holy spring spills and spills. Its rocky basin overflows.

Calypso's Island

Longing doubles the distances. Ulysses, wretched on the headlands—islanded, imprisoned, postponed—looks toward home where he imagines, after the last apple falls, after the last apple is pressed, he will hear again the shepherd's song, an intricate fugue of five notes as complex as a skein of lace.

For now, he breathes cedar and juniper smoke. Drinks freely from the island's four springs. He imagines a forest set before him, a sharp ax with an olive wood handle with which to cut and trim timbers to build a ship, a boat, a raft even. But for now, he broods and curses the vital winds that lift and fill no sails.

Before the Ceasefire

A cold scouring wind. Donkey hooves on stones. Mangled, rusted rebar ghosted in concrete dust. The morning star mute. Not a scrap to eat.

A Solace

A grid of fields. An ambiguous space between here and now. A cornflower in a cobalt bottle on the windowsill. The quality of light is what one recalls. Memory as spare as a spore. The beehives clustered like whitewashed buildings on a hillside. The swarm scattered through the airy woodland dense with wildflowers. What one calls the faraway is close and offers a solace hindsight rarely affords.

Lone Tree

Folks forced out; farmhouses, churches, and grain elevators abandoned amid vast square acreages the banks now own; hardly a crowd at the farm auction; a border collie barks at the auctioneer, whose over-amplified voice feedbacks when he gets too close to the microphone; all the buyers from out of town; locals stay clear; a last harvest for some; a future plowed under.

What Has Been Revealed

I struggle against time within it and desire for that unhindered by time. The tide approaches, the salt creek slows, stalls, then backs up. How to enter a way of knowing unknowingly, in innocence? How to move within, not against, the stasis? To welcome a stay, a reprieve from time? The tide continues. Advances. Withdraws. What sort of knowing exists outside change, beyond the flux? As waves retreat, sandpipers rush forward to claim what has been revealed, scurry away as water returns.

: :

Again, the child says, and again, I read the book. After noon, the day diminishes, the sun arched toward setting, downward. And again, the story ends. The story begins as it does again. As it did the first time. In and out of time at once.

Adagios of Islands

Between two days, days neither foreseen nor recollected—normal days—one props haphazardly a night.

: :

The moon is off-white, matte, deckled, like paper made from mulberry bark. The moon scuds on undulant waves.

: :

From a door ajar, light fans out, creates an intermediate space, a transparent veil on which to trip.

: :

The nuance of blues: sun-bleached, salt-faded, the false-blue of the corsage left to wilt in its clear, plastic clamshell.

: :

Shelter is a bit of space claimed amid the immensity. One needs a little shelter. A crust of bread. A sip to quench the thirst.

: :

Rumpled pillow, a tangle of bedsheets, captured as velvety shadows and stark whites, as the privacies to which they allude.

: :

The mirror conceals no likeness, holds no storage. A depthless, uncertain ground. What is longing but the half-remembered?

Awaiting the Reversal of the Poles

Magnetic north wanders like I do, lost, snow-blind, the idea of direction a mere idea, a construct, an abstraction which I attempt to apply to the blank dimension I am marooned in. I step but do not move. My position is a probability. I feel exhausted, the exhaustion of probabilities.

Nowhere Near Pie Town

Below the high desert mesa, a fertile valley. Coyote pace out beyond piñon juniper and mesquite. One could measure here subtle tectonics with the proper sensitivity, which the pronghorn must possess, as camouflaged, hidden, they stand en masse and with bounding strides, flee across the Lightning Field.

Without Coordinates or Scale

Yesterday is a grub dug up. Pale. Unchanged. The hard part remains: the chore of bereavement, the embodiment of grief, sorrow's unmeasurable weight and density. Smoke from wet wood. Sulfur and lilac. A stain. The past fixed with vinegar and salt. Without coordinates or scale: the far and the foreground out of focus.

A Tomb for Yannis Ritsos

If I were not this far inland, the one light left on in an upper room across the valley's dark expanse might be a dim lantern on a fishing boat. Like you, my friend, I wear shoes to sleep. The distances I travel at night are rugged. Eroded. The incline steep.

Nearsighted, I cannot read the future. Half-deaf, I miss half of what the oracle has to say. One star flickers on. Then off. There's the acrid, unkempt scent of a kerosene flame snuffed out when, at last, day breaks.

Moss Sutra

The thread of a sutra is like a melody tangled around a drone, the sigh of night wind in a moss temple, scripture, a field of tensions, a moment's oscillations, a quiver of logic, shallow shadows wet with moss on flagstones, a grammar.

Seemingly Arbitrary

He claims that his poems are collaged from the dictionary, a mere rearranging, a cutting and pasting. Child's play. But as his memory diminishes, he finds himself looking up words to reassure himself of their meaning. Soon he finds himself looking up the words in the definitions of the words he is looking up. Each word opaque. Page-bound. He does not know what to make of all the tiny, precise, and seemingly arbitrary illustrations.

A Passion

In the pent-up drama of a staged scene, the dead body is placed at an oblique angle to the audience. Those in charge of the body have been given a set of provisional procedures, ointments and spices. They touch the body tenderly as they never did when it was alive. The preparation gives way to sobs and whispers. The house lights go up and after the audience has mostly departed, a fisherman enters from stage left and tugs a tattered net with which to wrap the body and drag it matter-of-factly offstage.

Surface Tension

A raven, masked as a plague doctor, collects in a pouch seeds from lupine, milkweed, morning glory, bittersweet, indigo, and hollyhock. From nowhere near, a storm gathers. Dissipates. Re-gathers. The mountains pull down rain which falls on the river bend's cottonwoods. There beyond the range of hearing: a sharp beak preens the future's sleek feathers, pares away at the past.

A Nest Woven of Oak Trunks

after Andy Goldsworthy

What hand set down this tomb's first stone, that holds him as in a cradle: an exhausted stowaway in a dream? Delayed, he recollects the long history of displacements, a recursive passage, a labyrinth, the anticipated impasse of a soliloquy: unanswered, unanswerable. He sleeps beneath a woven nest of oak trunks set upside down as a roof above the tomb, a tomb with an open door, stairs up and out, a portal in a long stone wall, but to where?

As I Look On, the Tracks in the Snow Vanish

Hard to get away from where I stand, in the midst, without beginning or end. *There* I might seem displaced, dispersed, scattered. But I am *here*. The infinite is not permanence, but flux: additions and subtractions—multiplied and divided in harmony. Dusk like half-remembered womb-dark. *I* as a placeholder for the mind's paths and divagations. Ahead, the night's icy grove is carved out by headlights. I strike a match as an offering then blow it out. I mumble words now and then that float upon a disheveled grammar I call prayer.

Ain't It Just like the Night to Play Tricks When You're Trying to be so Quiet

All the while it was worthwhile, in a space of time, to cause time to pass in quiet, which is never quite complete, altogether, or wholly a quietude, a rest, a repose, a tranquility, or an absence of commotion. If only I could abnegate all exercise of the will, and purely, passively meditate on God and divine things. But it's easier to remain at rest, to acquiesce. Say a prayer, perhaps for the repose of the dead. To put on Mozart's *Requiem*. Interrupt the silence and coyly quit the quiet.

Still Life with Exterior

The table tipped, it seems, so that gravity accumulates in the foreground. A supplely draped cloth spills over the edge. Objects arranged on the broad flat surface, isolated except by how shadows touch, postpone, for now, the ephemeral. The day, a formidable vastness shaped by light, is washed away by dusk.

Beyond the window, a field of stones harvested to enclose within a stonewall the field. A moon sliver afloat in the pond's silver.

At Bull Run

Root wads. Lichen-ridden downed trunks. Light skids on water where wind roughs. When the cutbank collapses, a crow lumbers up into half-hearted flight. Where sun breaks through the canopy, an oblong circle of bluebells. Glare and shade flicker, reveal the warp and weft, the interwoven. The silence is encumbered by a minimal arrangement of tones—a quick revel of echo coming into focus or just slipping away. What we call *birdsong*. Each sound dulled by the swampy, cold, acidic soil, by a distance rimmed by hills.

An Errant Errand

One by one memories evaporate, change form, lift away, are shed somehow, lost. One departs from the screen into a lost field. The silence is complicated by all that keeps it from being silence: a caesura marked by empty space.

Wind-blown embers carry a precarious future. One dwells, abides in a book, a book not yet finished: drafty, a bright blue tarpaulin for a roof. Enchanted, enamored, one prays for the slyness of jackals, the shyness of fawns.

Within the confines of a plot, one toggles back and forth between the suspended moments. A comet foretells tumult: opulent magic stifled, a salamander as an embodied flame, lithium tarnishing in evaporation ponds. Before the soul is shaped, it dwells in a gray realm unknown to the spectrum.

One wakes within the chamber of a camera obscura, with only one's shadow as bedclothes, to the outside projected inside, upside down, as if one had slept on the ceiling. As if incised by a scrimshander, enough stars to suggest the *not-yet-counted*, the *infinite*. One closes one's eyes and hears the seep of starlight into stone.

As Syllable from Sound

A wisp of cloud quivers on the pond surface. Far is the drag of ink at a brushstroke's end. The skull, a rudimentary attic, houses the mind. I claim, nevertheless, to be of half a mind. The distance traversed is marked by an eddy of ellipses. I hear rain on the foxgloves, a watery gamelan. I wonder, wander, am waylaid; I retreat into melancholy. I am like a book, face-down, splayed. Like a moth about to take flight. I forget the aphorisms of amnesia and hide behind a door held tight with a hook and eye.

: :

I long for the mind to be more than the murk of an unmemorable nocturne, the mind, for a moment, coherent, unsullied. The debris jettisoned. I long for the ephemeral to extend its shelf life, to somehow remain as it flees, if only fleetingly. A willow's purple shadow levels the uneven ground where a ragged hedgerow marks the property line, the limits of *here*. I proceed with a blindfold and a dictionary, a magician kept company by spells and magic, by a sleight of hand.

: :

One hears a whirlpool before seeing it, the rush of the vortex inward and down, a self engulfing self, consumed, regenerated, without end, as if a prayer might compose a mind composed solely of prayer. Consider for now the candor of Jesus's body—a clumsy length of dead weight—flung across the old woman's lap to be held up awkwardly, embraced, wept-upon. A body marked. Gouged. Bruised. Breathless.

: :

I enter a story laden with prophecies. With an approximation of a translation, I depart ill-prepared. Does a souvenir preserve a past or mark a loss? I make notes, notations, scribbles, and doodles. Deboss, scratch, and tear the paper. As I watch the refugees prohibited from landing or wading to shore, I recall the tentative nature of shelter. My breath is out of sync. In Bruegel's "Magpie on the Gallows," the gallows form a gateway. To hear the magpie, I turn the radio knob slowly back and forth to find the right frequency. Time and space overlap. Each distorts the other. The burl, a scar, records an encounter. I touch distance without arrival. I wait to be fetched. To be called back.

Notes on the new poems in section II

The title, "A Dithering of Presences" is a phrase from Wallace Stevens's essay "A Collect of Philosophy."

In the poems, "A Tomb for Hart Crane," "A Tomb for Wallace Stevens," and "A Tomb for Yannis Ritsos," the idea of a poem as a tomb is borrowed, of course, from Stephane Mallarmé.

"A Tomb for Wallace Stevens" riffs upon language from the first and the last cantos of Wallace Stevens's poem "The Auroras of Autumn."

"Aperture" is in response to a dance performance called "Aperture" by Doug Varone and Dancers in 2023.

The title "Keep Your Lamp Trimmed and Burning," is borrowed from the song, "Keep Your Lamp Trimmed and Burning," first attributed to Blind Willie Johnson, who recorded it in 1928.

In "Enthusiasms," the language from Pablo Neruda is from his *100 Love Sonnets*, number *17*.

The title "Adagios of Islands" is a phrase from Hart Crane poem "Voyages."

"Moss Sutra" borrows its title from a 2010-2015 painting by Brice Marden, "Moss Sutra with the Seasons" which is in the collection of the Glenstone Museum in Potomac, Maryland.

"A Nest Woven of Oak Trunks" is in response to Andy Goldsworthy's "The Oak Room," at the Chateau La Coste in Provence.

The title "Ain't It Just like the Night to Play Tricks When You're Trying to be so Quiet" is from the opening of Bob Dylan's song "Visions of Johanna."

The poem, "An Errant Errand" was written in a collaboration with the visual artist, Jill Moser, for her *Talking Pictures* project.

The title, "As Syllable from Sound," is a phrase from Emily Dickinson 1862 poem which ends:

> The Brain is just the weight of God—
>
> For—Heft them—Pound for Pound—
>
> And they will differ—if they do—
>
> As Syllable from Sound—

Acknowledgments

The book's epigraph is from Gaston Bachelard's *L'Eau et les rêves: Essai sur l'imagination de la metière* (1942)

I would like to thank all the book editors with whom I have worked over forty-some years: Harry Ford at Atheneum and Alfred A. Knopf, Chase Twitchell at Ausable Books, Jon Thompson and David Blakesley at Free Verse Editions/Parlor Press, Daniel Slager at Milkweed Editions, Luke Hankins at Orison Books, Susannah Appelbaum at Codhill Press, and Gregory Wolfe at Slant Books for their generous attention to the poems here which first appeared in books they edited and brought into the world.

Many thanks to the editors of the following journals who first gave a home to the new poems here.

Amsterdam Review: "Errors in Continuity"

Elsewhere: "Of the Epic One Recalls a Passage"

Fence: "Backward to Zero"

Free State Review: "Walking Mike One Winter Day"

Georgia Review: "The House"

Hampden-Sydney Poetry Review: "A Tomb for Wallace Stevens"

Kestrel: "Without Coordinates or Scale"

The Laurel Review: "Remain Seated for the Duration"

Michigan Quarterly Review: "River Ice"

Plume: "Arcana"

Salvation South: "An Arrangement," "Keep Your Lamps Trimmed and Burning"

Southern Poetry Review: "Surface Tension"

Superpresent: "Lone Tree," "A Room at the Palace"

Trampset: "Katabasis"

Wallace Stevens Journal: "Mr. and Mrs. Stevens"

Witness: "The Turquoise Trail"

Permissions

Eric Pankey, "Returning in Winter," "How to Sustain the Visionary Mode," "Comes a Time," "A Confessional Poem," "The Anniversary," "Improvisation," and "The Constellations of Autumn" from *The Pear as One Example: New and Selected Poems 1984-2008*, copyright © 2008 by Eric Pankey. Reprinted with the permission of The Permissions Company, LLC on behalf used of Copper Canyon Press, coppercanyonpress.org. All rights reserved.

Eric Pankey,"Dismantling the Angel," "The Kingdom of Smoke," "The Talismanic Shirt," "The Autobiography of Fire," "The Parable of the Empty Jar," "Essay on Mannerism," "Essay on a Lemon," "Lunar Calendar," "The Equilibrium of a Swan's Feather," "Film Still," "Two Children Threatened by a Nightingale," "Owl," "The Blindfold," and "Essay on Compassion," originally published in *Dismantling the Angel*, copyright © 2014. Used by permission of Parlor Press.

Eric Pankey, "*Ars Poetica*," and "Souvenir de Voyage," from Augury (Minneapolis: Milkweed Editions, 2017). Copyright © 2017 by Eric Pankey. Reprinted with the permission of Milkweed Editions, milkweed.org.

Eric Pankey, "The Last Sunday in Lent," "Another Reading," "Melancholia," "Parable with my Father as a Boy," "A Public Education," "Book of Hours," "Trouble in Mind," and "Sanctuary," from *Owl of Minerva*. (Minneapolis: Milkweed Editions, 2019). Copyright © 2019 by Eric Pankey. Reprinted with the permission of Milkweed Editions, milkweed.org.

Eric Pankey, "Variations on Hadrian's 'Animula,'" "The Work of Poetry or An Imaginary Pane of Glass Parallel to Sea Level" and "On the Occasion of *The Release of the Senate Torture Report*," originally published in *Vestiges*, copyright © 2019. Used by permission of Parlor Press.

Eric Pankey, "Alias," "Outtakes from *The Newlywed Game*," "The Other Story about José," "Speed Dating," "False Sermon—True Story," "The Unexpected Returns," "By Another Route," "From This Day Forward," "The Hyenas," "A Slipknot as it Slips," "Romantic Landscape with the Garden of Gethsemane," "The School Nurse," and "Study for a Ghost," originally published in *Alias*, copyright © 2020 Used by permission of Parlor Press.

Eric Pankey, "Landscape in Theory: A Meditation" copyright © 2021 by Eric Pankey. Reprinted from *Not Yet Transfigured* by permission of Orison Books, Inc. All rights reserved.

Eric Pankey, "Eurydice," "No One Treats You Like a Mother When Your Mother is Dead," "Recently Recovered Pages from *The Complete List of Everything*," "The River Still Ragged with Ice Floes," "Buried for Now," "The Boredom that Precedes the Rapture," "Lilith," "The Weight," "The Spectrum's Violet End," "Border Crossing," "Oblique Strategies," and "The Sick Boy," originally published in *The History of the Siege*, copyright © 2024. Used by permission of Codhill Press.

Eric Pankey, "A Sonatina for Mark Strand," originally published in *Vanishments*, copyright © 2025. Used by permission of Slant Books.

XI
V
IX
VII